DIRTY
GOURMET

DIRTY GOURMET

FOOD FOR YOUR OUTDOOR ADVENTURES

AIMEE TRUDEAU

EMILY NIELSON

MAI-YAN KWAN

SKIPSTONE

dirty GOURMET

Published by Skipstone, an imprint of Mountaineers Books
Printed in China
24 23 22 21   6 7 8 9

Copyeditor: Nancy W. Cortelyou, Saffron Writes
Cover and book design: Jen Grable
Cover photographs: Clockwise from top left: *Pineapple Sake Cooler*; *A well-built campfire* (photo by Ryan Robert Miller); *Noodles with Spicy Peanut Sauce* Bottom: *Campfire Bibimbap*
All photographs by Dirty Gourmet, unless otherwise credited. Photos on pages 58, 63, 66, and 100 and back cover (top) by Ryan Robert Miller; Photos on pages 10, 16, 71 (bottom), 178, 185, 187 (middle), 188 (middle), 227, 239, and 264 by Daniel Pouliot; Photo page 21 (middle) by Linda Trudeau

Library of Congress Cataloging-in-Publication Data
Names: Trudeau, Aimee, author. | Nielson, Emily, author. | Kwan, Mai-Yan, author.
Title: Dirty gourmet : food for your outdoor adventures / Aimee Trudeau, Emily Nielson, and Mai-Yan Kwan.
Description: Seattle, Washington : Skipstone, [2018] | Includes bibliographical references and index.
Identifiers: LCCN 2017045775 (print) | LCCN 2017047755 (ebook) | ISBN 9781680511307 (ebook) | ISBN 9781680511291 (pbk)
Subjects: LCSH: Outdoor cooking. | LCGFT: Cookbooks.
Classification: LCC TX823 (ebook) | LCC TX823 .T78 2018 (print) | DDC 641.5/78—dc23
LC record available at https://lccn.loc.gov/2017045775

Printed on FSC-certified materials

ISBN (paperback): 978-1-68051-129-1
ISBN (ebook): 978-1-68051-130-7

Skipstone books may be purchased for corporate, educational, or other promotional sales, and our authors are available for a wide range of events. For information on special discounts or booking an author, contact our customer service at 800-553-4453 or mbooks@mountaineersbooks.org.

Skipstone
1001 SW Klickitat Way, Suite 201
Seattle, Washington 98134
206.223.6303
www.skipstonebooks.org
www.mountaineersbooks.org

CONTENTS

ON THE TRAIL

CAR CAMPING

BACKCOUNTRY CAMPING

RECIPE INDEX

INTRODUCTION

We want to see more people enjoying the wild outdoor spaces of the world. All three of us have had an adventure (or a thousand) that helped us realize how essential it is to get outside. We've heard all of the excuses, and made most of them ourselves, but we also know that getting started is the hardest part. You'll never regret a trip that leaves you dirty because it will also leave you empowered and full of stories to tell friends when you get home. You'll find yourself out there.

And then there's food. Many people spend time and energy planning every detail of their outdoor adventure but then treat food as an afterthought. For some, food is a roadblock to going on a trip at all. But it doesn't have to be this way. We firmly believe that food is an essential part of your outdoor experience. By taking it beyond just what you need to survive and using it for comfort and happiness, you can transform food into a significant part of a journey's memory, putting the cherry on top of that life-changing experience you went out there to have in the first place. And we want to help!

This book is not for one particular type of outdoorsperson. We want all of you—from the first-time family camper to the seasoned trekker—to feel confident planning for your specific trip's needs. Our recipes are based on simple formulas (in most cases), and are often vegetarian, because these are the most reliable type of recipes to work with when you have to think about things like perishability.

There will be challenges. You may forget a key ingredient or get rained out one day. Rather than despair, feel pride in the adaptations that your flexibility and creativity bring to these unplanned moments, and gain the confidence that self-reliance brings. If you make food part of the experience of being outdoors, the wilderness can be your comfort zone.

FOOD PHILOSOPHY

Food is an essential part of survival, comfort, warmth, and happiness. When we spend time outside, we get to experience an awareness of basic survival needs that is easily overlooked at home. In the backcountry, it is a big deal if you forget to bring your lunch. Most of us have a personal story of falling apart and struggling to function and being confused as to why, only to eat a little snack and be cured. This power of food is great. It's no wonder that the word "hangry" is in our vernacular.

In this book, we focus on healthy food, but that doesn't mean you won't see Sausage and Beer Mac and Cheese or Chocolate Pudding Cake in here. Healthy to us means real, whole foods that you cook yourself, rather than low calorie and low fat. Calories and fat can be your best friends on a cold day in the mountains.

Between the three of us, our families' roots are Southern, Chinese, French-Canadian, and Indian, and we all currently live in Southern California. This means you will see a lot of diversity in the foods and flavors in our recipes. We keep things simple when we can, and note sources for specialty items where needed.

LEAVE NO TRACE: STEWARDSHIP FOR OUTDOOR SPACES

Leave No Trace (LNT) ethics are extremely important to preserving the beauty of our world's outdoor spaces, and should be followed for all types of camping. Cooking brings up a lot of potential LNT concerns, so we discuss the most notable considerations in each chapter. Many campgrounds have amenities such as dumpsters, running water, and established fire rings that make it easier to follow LNT guidelines.

Everything you do in a camping situation affects the future visitors of that area. For instance, setting up a tent on delicate wildflowers means those flowers will not be there for the next person. Feeding a squirrel by leaving an orange peel on the ground may seem harmless—orange peels are biodegradable, right?—but that squirrel will go tell all of her friends to come back looking for more food near your camp tomorrow, and eventually create a pest problem. If this happens too often, the wildlife that shows up can be of a bigger and more dangerous variety. Unfortunately, there are already places where wild animals have little fear of humans and great knowledge of the delicious things we bring camping. This is bad for us and them.

On the other hand, picking up trash left behind by someone else ensures a better experience for the next person (keep in mind that this future camper could be you). This is a great activity for kids, so they get used to the idea of helping keep natural spaces clean and safe. We often play the game that whoever picks up a piece of trash from the trail gets to give it to someone else to carry out. This is a fun way to keep everyone (not just the kids!) focused on spotting trash throughout the day.

While Leave No Trace is really quite simple, it is not practiced often enough. As more and more people enjoy their public lands, the effects of use are becoming increasingly noticeable. Please familiarize yourself with the details of this philosophy at https://LNT.org before heading out on your next trip—and share what you learn with others out there. We'll do our part here by showing you how to plan your meals so you, too, can leave no trace.

HOW TO USE THIS BOOK

This book is organized first by the type of adventure—day trips, car camping, and backcountry camping—and then by meal type.

On the trail recipes can be prepared in advance at home or often at camp before heading out for the day, and are foods meant to be eaten straight out of a backpack or a cooler without much, if any, preparation on the trail. We keep in mind that the ingredients, pre-prepared or not, should generally be able to withstand half a day squished into a backpack. This section includes recipes for single-day trips or trail meals on a car camping or backcountry excursion.

Car camping recipes are closest in context to cooking in your home kitchen—and just as satisfying. Recipes in this section contain perishables and assume there is a car nearby chock full of gear. Methods employ either a two-burner camp stove or the grate of a campfire, which allows you to cook like you do on a home stovetop without much alteration. A Dutch oven in the coals allows you to bake. Bringing a cooler gives you access to some perishable ingredients that can expand your offerings. We keep these recipes simple in terms of steps, dishes, or ingredients and focus on using a whole portion of something rather than a part—or at least recommend when it's possible to do so. The recipe's method usually suggests how to prepare part of the dish at home, such as measuring out dry ingredients for biscuits into a ziplock bag or pre-chopping vegetables. If you don't have the time or interest to do this, you can still make all recipes from scratch at camp.

Backcountry recipes anticipate the concerns of weight, space, and temperature when exploring the unlimited trails that take you off the beaten path. They also fulfill the need for quick and easy meals after a long day hauling a pack up the trail. These recipes require the most specialized equipment out of the three categories. Your gear doesn't need to be fancy or expensive, but having

a lightweight stove with good simmer control offers the most versatility for executing any type of backcountry cooking you desire and deserve.

The Car Camping and Backcountry Camping sections each include an individualized **base kit** of tools needed (see specific chapters). These list the supplies to have ready to go at all times, which makes getting ready for your trip easier and prevents you from forgetting an essential. Most recipes also include an additional short list of **tools** that are used at camp. In this way, the recipe is written as a packing list. Note that tools used at home are not on either list. **Icons** (see "Cooking Method Legend" below) indicate the appropriate cooking method(s) for each recipe to help you narrow down the best recipes for your trip's amenities.

COOKING METHOD LEGEND

 Make at Home Virtually all of our On the Trail recipes are *Make at Home*. While some parts of recipes in other sections include *At Home* prep options, the recipes labeled with this icon are the only ones fully prepared at home.

 Two-burner Stove: These recipes need the versatility and stability of a traditional car camping stove, which most closely mimics a home stovetop.

 Campfire: Campfire recipes allow you to avoid bringing a stove altogether. The campfire can be used in several different ways, and specific instructions are included in these recipes.

 Lightweight Backpacking Stove: Backcountry recipes are often one-pot meals so a lightweight backpacking stove—almost always single burner—is all that's necessary for recipes with this icon.

ON THE TRAIL

Eating in the outdoors doesn't always happen in the coziness of a campsite. A lot of it happens on the trail, on a rock, or even in the dirt next to your car. Altitude, sun exposure, and physical exhaustion can intensify the need to have ready-to-eat food handy before symptoms become dangerous. Day trip needs can sneak up on us; since there is less preparation necessary than for a bigger overnight trip, it is surprisingly easy to leave home or camp underprepared for what lies ahead.

BASICS

Deceptively simple-sounding, trail food planning can be the most difficult: you need to have the energy to do it *before* you leave, and it can be challenging to predict how much food you'll want or need, or what will hold up best in your pack.

Most of these recipes are sturdy and stay fresh for at least half of a day, and they incorporate a lot of nutritional needs in only a few elements. Keep in mind that some of these recipes require using at-home tools, such as a food processor or blender.

Snacks are broken into "sweet" and "salty" categories, because a mix of both is generally welcomed on a trip. We tend to love hearty grain or bean-based salads for lunch, but there's also a great recipe on how to make a backpack-pressed sandwich if that's more your trail style.

Everyone has different caloric needs, and every trip has a different set of considerations, including activity levels and weather. Typically, our rule of thumb is that you need about 100 calories per hour during activities, on top of the calories from your regular meals. Keep in mind that you may want different things on the trail than you enjoy at home. For example, even though you may rarely eat sweet things at home, there's a chance you'll crave fruity, sugary snacks on high cardio days.

Fruit leather is great for this! Or, the pendulum may swing toward wanting saltier snacks than usual. Our Indian Spice Snack Mix (see Savory Snacks) is perfect for these days.

Get to know yourself and make sure you'll be happy with the food you bring for whichever activity you've made time for in your life. It may feel like more of an effort than grabbing a fast food burrito on the way out of town, but you will thank yourself when you have a satisfying homemade meal to keep you going. Then you can eat that burrito for dinner with a beer on the way home instead.

HOW TO PACK FOR A DAY TRIP

Trail recipes can be tricky to pack if all you are carrying is a small, overstuffed backpack. Hard, leakproof containers are the easiest thing to use for most recipes. Remember to pack an appropriate utensil for the meal, and always bring a napkin or bandana to help with cleanup. Bringing an extra ziplock bag or trash bag is helpful too so you don't have to put any soiled items back into the main compartment of your pack.

If the weather is exceptionally hot or the recipe is sensitive to the food safety "danger zone" (39° to 140° F), ice packs or personal coolers can help. Avodiablo is an example of a recipe that benefits from being kept cool. Build a little cooler inside your bag by adding an ice pack to a ziplock bag, and putting your food container inside. If you have the option of returning to your car for a midday break, just stash everything in a full-sized cooler. At break time, enjoy lunch complete with a picnic blanket or even a couple small chairs to enhance your comfort level.

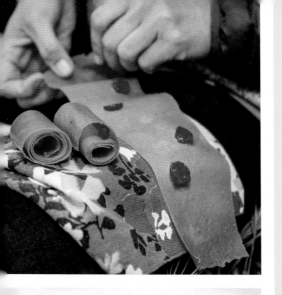

RECIPES

SAVORY SNACKS

SWEET SNACKS

MEALS

Indian Spice Snack Mix

Yield: 8 to 10 servings
Prep Time: 10 minutes
Cook Time: 1 hour

½ cup butter

2 teaspoons mustard seeds, whole

1 teaspoon fennel seeds, whole

1 teaspoon cumin seeds, whole

½ teaspoon cayenne pepper

½ teaspoon curry powder

½ teaspoon kosher salt

3 cups Wheat Chex

3 cups Corn Chex

3 cups lightly crushed, plain, ridged potato chips

½ cup pepitas

½ cup dry roasted peanuts

1 cup raisins

I live for Chex Mix. I've always loved it. As a kid, I had a sort of snack exchange with my best friend, Anne. I'd get her Twizzlers, and she'd get me Chex Mix. We'd eat our treats while canoeing in the lake in my backyard, either fishing or waiting for my dad to take us tubing behind his boat. The packaged stuff was pretty good, but homemade was the best. I've since taken over my own Chex Mix supply, expanding to include some different flavor combinations, like this Indian-inspired version. —*Emily*

Preheat the oven to 250° F.

In a roasting pan, add the butter, seeds, cayenne, curry powder, and salt. Stir together. Bake until toasted and fragrant, about 10 to 15 minutes.

Add both the cereals, chips, pepitas, and nuts, and stir well to coat with the spice mixture. Bake for 45 to 60 minutes, stirring every 15 minutes. Add in the raisins during the last 15-minute stirring interval.

Let cool and store in an airtight container.

Spicy Tofu Jerky

Yield: 4 servings

Prep Time: 1 hour

Cook Time: 2 hours

1 (14-ounce) block extra-firm tofu

FOR THE MARINADE

½ cup low-sodium soy sauce

1 tablespoon maple syrup

1 teaspoon smoked paprika

1 teaspoon cayenne pepper

1 teaspoon brown sugar

1 teaspoon liquid smoke

¼ teaspoon Worcestershire sauce

¼ teaspoon freshly ground black pepper

One of the things I miss out on as a vegetarian camper is jerky. It's a great way to add protein to your diet without worrying about perishability. Jerky is a welcome savory snack among the many sweet ones that are readily available and it can also be eaten as part of a meal. There are some pretty good vegetarian alternatives, but they aren't always easy to find and they definitely don't taste as good as this tofu jerky. There's no need for a dehydrator; this recipe is made in the oven. If you are vegetarian, make sure to look for vegetarian Worcestershire sauce, as it usually contains fish. I think of this recipe as a "gateway" to tofu, so even if you typically avoid tofu, it's worth a try. —*Aimee*

Press the tofu by wrapping it in a towel and placing a heavy object on top of it. (I like to use my cast iron skillet.) Press for about 30 to 45 minutes, until tofu becomes firmer and dryer.

Meanwhile, make the marinade. In a large bowl, combine the soy sauce, syrup, paprika, cayenne, brown sugar, liquid smoke, Worcestershire, and pepper. Whisk together to mix well.

Cut the tofu into very thin slabs, about ⅛-inch thick. (I prefer them to be unevenly cut so the tofu looks more like jerky and the textures vary.) Place the tofu strips in the marinade and make sure each piece is sufficiently covered. Let sit in the marinade bowl for at least 30 minutes, and up to overnight.

When you're ready to bake the tofu, preheat the oven to 300° F.

Arrange the tofu strips in a single layer on a rimmed baking sheet and bake for 2 to 3 hours, until the tofu has become dark, thick, and chewy. The tofu will get firmer as it cools, so remove it from the oven a few minutes before you think the texture is perfect.

Store in an airtight container and keep chilled until ready to serve.

SPICY TOFU JERKY

SAVORY GRANOLA (PG 26)

Savory Granola

Yield: About 5 cups

Prep Time: 5 minutes

Cook Time: 45 minutes

2 cups rolled oats

2 cups packed, chopped fresh kale

1 cup toasted sunflower seeds

1 cup toasted pepitas

2 tablespoons black sesame seeds

⅓ cup extra-virgin olive oil

¼ cup honey

¾ teaspoon kosher salt

¼ teaspoon cayenne pepper

½ teaspoon freshly ground black pepper

When I worked for REI, I experienced savory granola for the first time. I met up with a friend at a cycling training event who shared hers with me. What a nice alternative to the typical sweet granola! For this book, we experimented with a few different sweet recipes but with a savory twist, and this was the clear winner.

If you've never made kale chips, you're in for a treat. This recipe includes the flavor of kale chips but with some added calories and health benefits from the other ingredients. I leaned toward more spice in this recipe, but turn the heat up or down depending on your preferences. Because it doesn't use that much sugar, this granola is more crumbly than clumpy, so it doubles as a great topping for something like soup. —*Emily*

Preheat the oven to 325° F.

In a large bowl, mix the oats, kale, sunflower seeds, pepitas, and black sesame seeds.

In a small bowl, mix the oil and honey. Add the salt, cayenne, and pepper to the oil and honey mixture. Pour the oil mixture over the oat mixture, and stir to completely coat.

Pour the granola onto a rimmed baking sheet, spreading it out evenly (but you don't have to be too careful about it).

Bake for 30 to 45 minutes, stirring every 10 minutes. Granola is done when the oats start to turn brown and the kale crisps up. Let cool.

Store in an airtight container.

Pea Pesto Dip

Yield: 1½ cups
Prep Time: 10 minutes
Cook Time: 5 minutes

1 cup fresh or frozen peas

2 tablespoons walnuts

1 small clove garlic, peeled

½ cup packed basil

3 tablespoons extra-virgin olive oil

2 tablespoons Parmesan cheese, grated

¼ teaspoon kosher salt

¼ teaspoon freshly ground black pepper

FOR SERVING

Carrot sticks

Radishes

Crackers

We originally used this pea pesto combination as a spread for sandwiches but liked it so much that we upgraded it to serve as a dip as well. And what's not to love? There are only a few ingredients that take only 15 minutes to whip up. The peas are unexpected, and bring a freshness to the dip that a typical pesto doesn't possess. Serve it with raw veggies, crackers, and Swiss cheese for an instant picnic. *—Mai-Yan*

Prepare and set aside a bowl of ice water.

Fill a small pot with water, add a big pinch of salt, and bring to a boil. Add the peas to the boiling water and cook until they turn bright green, about 1 minute. Drain the peas and place them immediately in the prepared ice water to keep them from cooking further.

In the bowl of a food processor fitted with the metal blade attachment, place the walnuts and garlic, and process until finely chopped. Add the peas, basil, oil, Parmesan, salt, and pepper, and process until light and spreadable. If necessary, add a little water to achieve a dippable consistency. Taste and adjust seasoning as needed.

Store in an airtight container and keep chilled until ready to serve.

Shiitake Rice Balls

Yield: 8 to 10 rice balls

Prep Time: 30 minutes

Cook Time: 15 minutes

1 cup short grain white rice

2 cups water

3 scallions, finely chopped

2 teaspoons black or white sesame seeds, toasted

1/4 teaspoon kosher salt

FOR THE MUSHROOM FILLING

1/2 tablespoon vegetable oil

1 cup shiitake mushrooms, finely chopped

1 tablespoon soy sauce

1/2 teaspoon honey

I first tested this recipe on a hike up to the Mount Wilson Observatory. It was a really hot day, and although we were prepared with water and food, I wasn't prepared for the extreme steepness of the trail. To make matters worse, our group of five got separated, and we spent close to eight hours apart, only to reunite back at the car. This is a good reminder to review maps, and discuss protocol and emergency procedures as a group, before heading out on adventures—even if it's with people you usually venture out with. Luckily, all ended well and we enjoyed these delicious rice balls together as the sun set.

Rice balls, or *onigiri,* are a ubiquitous snack in Japan. They come in triangle or ball shapes, and can be stuffed with many different fillings, including spicy tuna and pickled plum. Our version is made with shiitake mushrooms and soy sauce for extra umami. The key to making these a little less labor intensive is to set out all your ingredients and bowls in the correct order before you start. Once you get going, you'll get the hang of it and your rice balls will get prettier with each try. Bonus: you can turn this snack into an appetizer at camp! Simply pan fry the rice balls in a nonstick skillet with a little oil until the rice gets crispy and golden brown.
—*Mai-Yan*

In a small pot, add rice and rinse with water, swirling it around a couple times before carefully draining out the water. Add 2 cups fresh water and bring to a boil over high heat. Reduce the heat to low and simmer, covered, for 15 minutes, or until the water is absorbed.

While rice is cooking, prepare the mushroom filling. Heat the oil in a skillet over medium-high heat. When it's hot, add the mushrooms. Cook on medium heat for 5 to 10 minutes, stirring occasionally. When the mushrooms are soft and lightly browned, remove from heat. Add the soy sauce and honey, mixing well. Transfer the mixture to a small bowl.

When the rice is cooked, transfer it from the pot to a large bowl, and let it cool until it is warm to the touch. Add the scallions, sesame seeds, and salt. Mix gently.

Prepare a small bowl of warm water with a healthy pinch of salt. Dip clean hands into the warm salted water and shake off any excess.

Using a wooden spoon or rice paddle, spread a palm-full of warm rice into one hand. Add 1 tablespoon of the filling in the middle. Fold up the rice around the filling. Pack the rice tightly with both hands, making a ball. Repeat with the remaining rice and filling.

To store, tightly wrap the rice balls in plastic wrap individually. Store the wrapped rice balls in an airtight container and refrigerate until you leave for your trip. These are best eaten at room temperature the same day they are made.

Variation: Spicy Tuna Rice Balls

In place of the mushroom filling above, drain a 5-ounce can of tuna. In a small bowl, mix the tuna with 3 table-spoons mayonnaise, 1 teaspoon sriracha, $\frac{1}{4}$ teaspoon freshly ground black pepper, and $\frac{1}{4}$ teaspoon kosher salt. Prepare as above using this filling to stuff into the rice balls.

SWEET SNACKS

Black Sesame Cashew Granola Brittle

Yield: About 5 cups

Prep Time: 10 minutes

Cook Time: 30 minutes

½ cup dark brown sugar

½ cup canola oil

¼ cup honey

½ teaspoon kosher salt

3 cups rolled oats

1 cup cashews

1 cup unsweetened coconut flakes

½ cup black sesame seeds

The first event we did as Dirty Gourmet was an art fair. Not so outdoorsy, but people were "hiking" around looking at and purchasing all sorts of art—and they got hungry doing it. We made several products to sell there, but the main thing people wanted to buy was our granola. We offered two flavors, and both sold out (and there was a wait list!).

This recipe is one of those two flavors. We've sold it a handful of times since then and it continues to be a favorite. The texture is much like brittle, starting off as big, irregular slabs. It is easy to eat like a bar, but it's not a big deal if it crumbles in your pack. —*Aimee*

Preheat the oven to 325° F.

Line a large rimmed baking sheet with a silicone mat or parchment paper. Set aside.

In a small saucepan, combine the brown sugar, oil, honey, and salt. Cook over low heat, stirring frequently, until the mixture is hot and just starts to bubble. Remove from heat.

In a large bowl, combine the oats, cashews, coconut flakes, and sesame seeds. Add the sugar mixture, stirring to coat.

Spread the mixture onto the prepared baking sheet and bake, stirring every 10 minutes, until the granola is golden (about 30 minutes). Remove from the oven and let cool completely.

Break brittle into large chunks and store in an airtight container.

Homemade Nut Butters

I'm a little obsessed with making my own nut butters. It's magical how you can throw whole nuts into a food processor and, through breaking down and releasing their oils, they turn into nut butter. Nut butter is dense with calories and full of nutrients, giving you a healthy energy boost when you're ready for a break. To package these for a hike, you can scoop the nut butter into a small airtight container, but a reusable squeeze tube works well too. —*Aimee*

Mocha Almond Butter

Yield: About 1 cup

Prep Time: 5 minutes

Cook Time: 15 minutes, plus 20 to 30 minutes for processing

1½ cups almonds

1 tablespoon coffee beans

1½ ounces dark chocolate

¼ teaspoon kosher salt

1 tablespoon powdered sugar (optional)

A few coffee beans blended into this Mocha Almond Butter give you a little caffeine boost, plus their bitterness balances out the sweetness of the chocolate. Roasting the almonds really helps them to release their oils in the food processor. If you don't roast them, your almonds may take significantly longer to turn into butter. This is lovely smeared on croissants while on an early morning hike.

Preheat the oven to 300°F.

Spread the almonds on a rimmed baking sheet and bake until they smell toasted, about 15 minutes.

In the bowl of a food processor fitted with the metal blade attachment, place almonds and coffee beans. Process for about 20 to 30 minutes, occasionally scraping down the sides of the processor bowl. You may also need to turn off your food processor and give it a break every few minutes to prevent it from overheating. (You might think it's never going to turn into nut butter, but keep going and eventually it will.) Once the mixture is smooth and creamy, add the chocolate and salt. Continue processing until it's smooth like butter. Taste and add powdered sugar, if desired. Cool slightly before packaging.

To package for a hike, scoop the nut butter into a small leakproof container.

Coconut Ginger Walnut Butter

Yield: ½ cup

Prep Time: 20 minutes

1 cup raw walnuts

4 tablespoons crystallized ginger chips, divided

2 tablespoons sweetened coconut flakes

⅛ teaspoon kosher salt

1½ tablespoons coconut oil

The walnuts lend a creamy element and the ginger gives this nut butter a little kick. It's great smeared on apples and bananas.

Preheat the oven to 300° F.

On a rimmed baking sheet, spread out the walnuts and bake until they smell toasted, about 10 minutes.

In the bowl of a food processor fitted with the metal blade attachment, place the walnuts, 3 tablespoons of the ginger, coconut flakes, and salt. Process for about 5 minutes, occasionally scraping down the sides of the processor bowl. The mixture should resemble a chunky paste. Add the coconut oil and blend until it's creamy. Add the remaining ginger, and process just until incorporated.

To package for a hike, scoop the nut butter into a small leakproof container.

Pistachio Almond Butter

Yield: About 1 cup

Prep Time: 5 minutes

Cook Time: 15 minutes, plus 20 to 30 minutes for processing

1 cup almonds

½ cup shelled roasted pistachios

¼ cup powdered sugar

1 tablespoon refined coconut oil or almond oil

1 teaspoon almond extract

¼ teaspoon kosher salt (omit if pistachios are salted)

This nut butter reminds me of pistachio ice cream. Spread it on cookies or dark chocolate. Note that most pistachios are roasted. If the ones you buy are not roasted, roast them with the almonds. Just like in the Mocha Almond Butter, roasting the almonds speeds up the process, so don't skip this step.

Preheat the oven to 300°F.

Spread the almonds on a rimmed baking sheet and bake until they smell toasted, about 15 minutes.

In the bowl of a food processor fitted with the metal blade attachment, place almonds and pistachios. Process for about 20 to 30 minutes, occasionally scraping down the sides of the processor bowl. (You might think it's never going to turn into nut butter, but keep going and eventually it will.)

Once the mixture is smooth and creamy, add the powdered sugar, oil, extract, and salt. Continue processing until it's smooth. Cool slightly before packaging.

To package for a hike, scoop the nut butter into a small leakproof container.

Piña Colada Fruit Leather

Yield: 8 strips, about 2 inches by 12 inches

Prep Time: 10 minutes

Cook Time: 3 hours

1 pineapple, cored and cut into chunks

2 tablespoons orange juice

1 (14-ounce) can coconut milk, unshaken

½ cup maraschino cherries, sliced in half

Fruit is one of the simplest things to dehydrate. Fruit leather is easy to make in an oven, a dehydrator, or even a hot car! This recipe is written for the oven just in case you don't own a dehydrator. Experiment with different fruits to create endless combinations.

This mix is one of our favorites because it balances sweet and tart flavors with coconut cream, which adds an extra special component. The color is nice and vibrant, especially with the addition of electric red maraschino cherries (you can, of course, swap these with "real" cherries or leave them out altogether if you aren't a maraschino fan). With a stocked cupboard of this healthier-than-most sweet snack, you'll be ready to run out of the house at a moment's notice—if that's how you "plan" your day trips. —*Emily*

Preheat the oven to its lowest setting, about 170° F.

Line a rimmed baking sheet with a silicone mat or wax paper. Set aside.

In a blender, combine the pineapple and orange juice. Open the can of coconut milk, scoop the cream off the top and into the blender. It should be about ¼ cup or so. Blend the mixture until it is pureed.

Place a medium saucepan over medium heat, add the fruit puree, and cook until it reduces by half, about 20 minutes. Remove from the heat when it measures about 2 cups.

Pour the mixture onto the prepared baking sheet. Tilt the sheet to all four corners to evenly cover it with the puree. Sprinkle the cherries across the top of the puree. Bake until tacky, checking for doneness every 30 minutes, about 2 to 3 hours.

Remove from the oven and let cool completely. Peel the sheet from the liner, and slice into strips. Stack strips with wax paper in between, or roll up each strip.

Store in an airtight container.

MEALS

Citrus Miso Quinoa Salad

Yield: 6 servings
Prep Time: 15 minutes
Cook Time: 15 minutes

1 cup quinoa
2 carrots, finely chopped
3 scallions, chopped
1 cup snap peas, chopped
1 cup red bell pepper, chopped
½ cup toasted almonds, chopped

FOR THE DRESSING
4 tablespoons orange juice
4 tablespoons rice vinegar
2 tablespoons white miso
2 tablespoons soy sauce
1 tablespoon toasted sesame oil

Mai-Yan and I are climbers, and we are lucky enough to live near Joshua Tree National Park—a world-class climbing area. We head out there as frequently as possible during climbing season, often just for a day trip. The park is huge, so no matter how much we try to limit our climbing plans to one location, we end up doing a bit of traveling. It allows us to come back to the car several times throughout the day, so we take advantage of having a cooler waiting for us. This Citrus Miso Quinoa Salad along with a cold drink makes the perfect snack for a short break or a picnic lunch in between climbs. —*Emily*

Cook the quinoa according to package directions. It should be fluffy with no water remaining in the pot. Transfer the quinoa to a large bowl, and let it cool completely.

Next, make the dressing. In a small bowl or jar, add the juice, vinegar, miso, soy sauce, and sesame oil, and mix well.

Once the quinoa is at room temperature, add the chopped vegetables and half of the dressing. Toss and add more dressing to taste.

Store in an airtight container.

Avodiablo

3 hard-boiled eggs, peeled and chopped

3 tablespoons mayonnaise

1 tablespoon chipotle pepper in adobo sauce

2 teaspoons yellow mustard

2 teaspoons sweet relish

1/4 teaspoon kosher salt

1/8 teaspoon paprika

2 small limes

4 ripe avocados

FOR THE GARNISH

2 green onions, chopped

2 tablespoons cilantro, chopped

My favorite thing about cookbooks is the delight that comes from finding a recipe that sounds like something I'd never like but making it anyway and discovering a new favorite recipe. The same goes for testing each other's recipes. Mai-Yan shared this, but I avoided it for weeks, thinking it sounded weird. But I do *love* deviled eggs, so I eventually tested it. And I can say it is one of the most exciting recipes in this book. It is a perfect little package that can be eaten without a plate, and it includes enough calories and protein to keep you going on an active day out. Some assembly is required on the trail, but a pocketknife, spoon, and napkins should do the trick. We recommend eating Avodiablo with tortilla chips, but if you forget them, it is just as delicious by itself. —*Emily*

AT HOME

In a small bowl, place the eggs, mayonnaise, pepper, mustard, sweet relish, salt, and paprika, and mix well. Transfer to an airtight container and keep chilled until ready to use.

If desired, prep the garnish, place in a ziplock bag, and keep chilled.

ON THE TRAIL

Cut the limes into quarters.

Cut the avocados in half and remove the pits. Make shallow hatch marks in each avocado half and squeeze lime juice onto each.

Spoon a generous amount of the egg mixture onto the avocado, and serve with tortilla chips.

Apple Oatmeal Breakfast Cookies

Yield: 12 (2- to 2½-inch) cookies

Prep Time: 10 minutes

Cook Time: 20 minutes

2 apples

¼ cup plus 1 teaspoon coconut oil

1 tablespoon maple syrup

1 large ripe banana

½ cup packed pitted dates

1 teaspoon vanilla extract

1 teaspoon baking powder

1 teaspoon cinnamon

½ teaspoon kosher salt

2 cups rolled oats

½ cup walnuts, roughly chopped

I struggle with the idea of breakfast cookies. On the one hand, I love the idea of eating cookies for breakfast, especially if they are healthy. On the other hand, most healthy recipes I've tried have resulted in heavy, unflavorful blobs of baked oatmeal. After many trials, I landed on this one, and it's so good. Sautéing the apples in coconut oil and maple syrup really brings out the flavor of the fruit, giving the cookie its distinct flavor. If the banana sounds strange with the apple, don't worry, because you can't taste it—it's just there as a binder. —*Aimee*

Preheat the oven to 350° F.

Peel and core one of the apples, then dice it.

In a small skillet over medium heat, heat 1 teaspoon of the coconut oil. Add the diced apple and sauté until slightly browned and cooked through, about 5 minutes. Add the maple syrup and stir to combine. Remove from heat and set aside.

Cut the other apple into large chunks, removing the core. (You don't need to peel it.)

In the bowl of a food processor fitted with the metal blade attachment, add the large apple chunks, ¼ cup of the coconut oil, banana, dates, and vanilla. Process until the mixture is relatively smooth, about 2 minutes. Add the baking powder, cinnamon, and salt to the mixture, and process again, just until the ingredients are combined. Add the rolled oats and pulse a few times, just until the oats are roughly chopped.

Transfer the oat mixture to a bowl. Stir in the sautéed apples and the walnuts.

Using a ¼-cup measuring cup, drop heaps of dough onto a rimmed baking sheet, about 2 inches apart.

Bake for about 17 to 18 minutes or until lightly browned on the edges. Cool slightly before transferring to a wire rack to cool completely.

Store in an airtight container.

AVODIABLO (PG 40)

LENTIL FARRO SALAD (PG 44)

OATMEAL BREAKFAST COOKIES (PG 41)

Lentil Farro Salad

Yield: 4 servings

Prep Time: 15 minutes

Cook Time: 20 to 30 minutes

1 cup green lentils, picked over and rinsed

1 cup farro

2 stalks of celery, diced

1 red bell pepper, diced

¼ cup fresh Italian parsley, minced

FOR THE VINAIGRETTE

½ cup extra-virgin olive oil

1 medium onion, diced

4 garlic cloves, minced

1½ teaspoons kosher salt, divided

½ cup red wine vinegar

1 tablespoon honey

1 teaspoon Dijon mustard

2 teaspoons oregano

1 teaspoon freshly ground black pepper

FOR SERVING

1 red bell pepper, cored with seeds removed, cut into 4 wedges

When Aimee and I went on a trans-Canadian bike tour, we met a quirky French guy named Bruno who ended up cycling with us for part of our journey. A few years later, I took him up on an offer to be a guest presenter at the annual bike touring festival he organizes in France. Bruno and his girlfriend, Marianne, picked me up at the airport, threw my boxed bike in the back of their pickup, and drove straight to Chamonix at the base of the French Alps. Despite my jet-lagged state, the sparkle of Mont Blanc in the distance and the swaying of all the paragliders in the sky impressed me. But what was even more impressive was the impromptu picnic that suddenly appeared before me. Marianne had prepared a simple lentil salad that was just what I needed at that moment—wholesome, tasty, and nourishing. Even if you can't get to Chamonix, you'll definitely feel fulfilled by this Lentil Farro Salad.

This recipe gets better with age. So, if you're one of those folks who plan ahead for your camping weekends, you can make this up to three days ahead. And if you're like us, and make too much food for your camping trips, this is a welcome treat when you return home starving on Sunday afternoon. —*Mai-Yan*

In a medium pot over high heat, bring 4½ cups of water to a boil. Once the water is boiling, add the lentils, farro, and a big pinch of salt, and return to a boil. Reduce heat to low, cover, and cook until the water is absorbed, about 20 to 25 minutes. The farro should be al dente and the lentils should be tender but still hold their shape. Drain the lentils and farro through a fine mesh strainer and transfer to a large bowl. Set aside.

Meanwhile, make the vinaigrette. First, caramelize the onion. Heat the oil in a large skillet over medium heat. Add the onion and stir to coat with the oil. Spread the onions evenly across the skillet and cook, stirring occasionally, making sure to keep the onions evenly spread. (You may need to reduce the heat to low in order to keep the onions from burning.) Cook until the onions are browned, about 20 to 30 minutes. Remove from heat and cool slightly. Transfer the onions and oil to a bowl.

Mince the garlic and then sprinkle 1 teaspoon of salt over the top of it. Gather the salted garlic into a pile and, holding your knife at a 30-degree angle to the board, scrape your knife across the board, smashing the garlic. Alternate between mincing and pressing until the garlic resembles a paste.

In the bowl with the onions, add the garlic paste, vinegar, honey, mustard, oregano, the remaining ½ teaspoon salt, and pepper. Stir or whisk the mixture vigorously until the vinaigrette ingredients are combined.

After the farro and lentils have cooled, add to the large bowl the celery, bell pepper, and parsley. Pour the vinaigrette over the mixture, and toss well. Taste and season with additional salt and pepper, as needed.

Divide the salad into four servings, and place each into a reusable bag or container, including a red bell pepper wedge with each serving. The wedge is your ultralight edible spoon (just don't forget a napkin)! Keep chilled until ready to serve.

Lemony Kale and Avocado Sandwich

Yield: 2 sandwiches

Prep Time: 5 minutes

2 leaves of kale

Grated zest of half a small lemon

Juice of 1 small lemon

2 tablespoons shredded Parmesan cheese

2 teaspoons extra-virgin olive oil

Kosher salt and freshly ground black pepper, to taste

2 sturdy sandwich rolls

1 avocado

This recipe evolved from a salad I make all the time at home. I tend to crave greens on the trail, and hearty ones like kale hold up even after sitting dressed in your bag all day. You can certainly eat the kale as a salad, but piled onto a sandwich roll with smashed avocado elevates it to a hearty trail meal. The kale won't wilt or bruise easily and it actually gets better over the course of a day or two in a salad or sandwich like this one. —*Aimee*

Tear kale into small pieces and place in a medium bowl.

Add the lemon zest and juice, Parmesan, and oil. Massage to coat the kale. Season with salt and pepper, to taste.

Smash one half of the avocado onto both sides of each sandwich roll. Top one side of the roll with the kale mixture and cover with the other side of the roll.

Store in an airtight container and keep chilled.

LEMONY KALE AND AVOCADO SANDWICH (PG 45)

PANCAKE SANDWICH

Pancake Sandwich

Yield: 4 sandwiches

Prep Time: 10 minutes

Cook Time: 20 minutes

FOR THE PANCAKES

1¼ cups milk

3 tablespoons vegetable oil, plus 2 to 3 tablespoons for cooking

1 large egg

1¼ cups all-purpose flour

2 teaspoons baking powder

½ teaspoon kosher salt

FOR THE SANDWICH FILLING

8 to 12 slices deli meat, such as turkey or Tofurky

4 leaves of romaine, washed, dried, and bottom trimmed

4 slices provolone cheese

½ to ¾ cup hummus

One of the best things about living in Los Angeles (besides the weather, of course) is its proximity to mountains *and* ocean. The next best thing is the abundance of food available: year-round fresh produce, authentic cuisine from all around the world, and food trucks at every other corner. This pancake sandwich idea actually came from a food truck that I stumbled upon in a "hangry" moment. If you need an excuse to eat pancakes beyond breakfast, here it is. Cook up that leftover batter and let the joy of breakfast trickle into the afternoon. —*Mai-Yan*

In a medium bowl, whisk together the milk, 3 tablespoons of the oil, and egg. Sift together the flour, baking powder, and salt, and then add this dry mixture to the wet ingredients. Whisk wet and dry ingredients together until just moistened. Do not overmix! A few small lumps are fine.

Heat 1 tablespoon of the oil in a skillet over medium heat. (Don't skimp on the oil, especially if your skillet is *not* nonstick.)

When the skillet is hot, pour ¼ cup batter into the skillet. Cook for 2 to 3 minutes or until the batter has little bubbles showing. Flip the pancake and cook for another 1 to 2 minutes, or until bottom is golden brown. Set aside to cool. Repeat with the rest of the batter, making 8 pancakes total.

Assemble a sandwich: Slather 2 to 3 teaspoons of hummus onto two pancakes. Pile one pancake with 2 to 3 slices of the deli meat, 1 lettuce leaf, and 1 slice of the cheese. Top the pile with the other pancake. Repeat with the rest of the pancakes.

Package the sandwiches in an airtight container and keep chilled. Bonus: pack an avocado (along with a pocketknife) to add more goodness to your sandwich on the trail.

Curried Chickpea Salad

Yield: 4 to 6 servings

Prep Time: 10 minutes

½ cup egg-free mayonnaise

Juice of 1 small lemon

1 tablespoon curry powder

¾ teaspoon garlic powder

½ teaspoon red pepper flakes

½ teaspoon kosher salt

½ teaspoon freshly ground black pepper

2 (14-ounce) cans chickpeas, drained

1 carrot, diced (about ½ cup)

2 scallions, sliced (about ½ cup)

½ cup raisins

FOR SERVING

Crackers or a bagel with crunchy lettuce

This hearty "salad" is reminiscent of one of my favorite dishes—curried *chicken* salad—but less perishable for warm weather outdoor activities. We swapped the chicken for chickpeas and used an egg-free mayonnaise as the dressing base. Egg-free mayo might sound unusual, but it is surprisingly easy to find nowadays. It really opens up the possibilities for including mayo in trail recipes. And trust us—as serious mayo lovers, we can assure you that it is just as delicious as the real thing. We love this salad on bagel halves with crisp romaine lettuce, or simply on crackers if you're nibbling throughout the day. It holds up to being squished into your backpack, right along with the rest of your Ten Essentials.
—*Emily*

AT HOME

In a large bowl, place the mayonnaise, lemon juice, curry powder, garlic powder, red pepper flakes, salt, and pepper, and mix well to combine. Add the chickpeas, carrots, scallions, and raisins, and stir to coat everything. Scoop into an airtight container and keep chilled until ready to use.

Make a sandwich if you'll be on the go, or eat it as a spread on crackers if you'll be near a more luxurious picnic spot.

CILANTRO JALAPEÑO PESTO

CARAMELIZED ONION SPREAD

SUN-DRIED TOMATO PESTO

Pressed Sandwich Formula

The ultimate portable meal is the sandwich, and the best type of sandwich to enjoy outdoors is one that is "pressed" in your backpack. We couldn't come up with a single favorite sandwich recipe, so we're presenting the idea as more of a formula. Here we showcase a few of our favorite spreads that can guide the theme of your sandwich and infuse flavor into whatever combination of ingredients you choose.

Once you've assembled your sandwiches before your trip, pack them at the bottom of your pack with a few small cooler packs around them, then let them get squished.

Bread: The most important factor in bread choice is sturdiness. The bread is what soaks up the flavor from all the other elements, so big holes on the inside are beneficial, but you also want a nice crust across the outside to hold it all together and prevent sogginess. Because you intentionally squish this sandwich in your pack, make sure the bread is a little thicker than you'll want it to be when it's ready to eat.

Protein: Protein can be tricky in terms of perishability on a hot day out with no cooler. Smoked or cured meats like salami or sausage are best, or choose no meat at all. Hard cheeses like Parmesan, dry jack, and extra-sharp cheddar add a little protein to the vegetarian option. Some of the spreads included here are made with ground nuts for creaminess and a boost of protein.

Vegetables: There are plenty of hardy vegetables that only get better as they hang out in your sandwich. Kale and collards are our favorite greens. Marinated roasted peppers, artichokes, mushrooms, onions, and olives are all good choices as well. Because our spreads add brightness that infuses the whole sandwich, there isn't a need for the more delicate veggies you may otherwise want to include.

Condiments: These spreads are super flavorful on their own so you don't really need other condiments. But if you like, choose non-perishable, non-soggy options such as mustard or hot sauce rather than mayonnaise or olive oil.

Sun-Dried Tomato Pesto

Yield: About 1 cup
Prep Time: 15 minutes

½ cup sun-dried tomatoes
½ cup cashews
¼ cup extra-virgin olive oil
¼ cup fresh Italian parsley
1 tablespoon balsamic vinegar
¼ teaspoon kosher salt
½ teaspoon freshly ground black pepper
Zest and juice of 1 small lemon

I *love* fresh tomatoes on my sandwiches, but they aren't easy to transport in a pack. Sun-dried tomatoes got tossed aside for a while but are experiencing another culinary moment. So we're taking advantage of it by enjoying this perfect-for-camping ingredient more often, and this Sun-Dried Tomato Pesto offers a way to get tomatoes' bright acidity back into my lunches. —*Emily*

AT HOME

In the bowl of a food processor fitted with the metal blade attachment, place tomatoes, cashews, oil, parsley, vinegar, salt, and pepper. Process until blended. (Little chunks are OK—you don't want it to become like tomato paste.)

Transfer mixture to a small lidded container. Stir in the zest and lemon juice. Adjust with more lemon juice and salt, to taste. Refrigerate until your trip.

Cilantro Jalapeño Pesto

Yield: About 1 cup

Prep Time: 5 minutes

½ cup almonds

1 bunch of cilantro, tough stems cut off

1 jalapeño, stemmed, seeded, and roughly chopped

2 cloves garlic, peeled

Juice of 1 lime

¼ teaspoon kosher salt

¼ teaspoon freshly ground black pepper

⅓ cup extra-virgin olive oil

One of the best sandwiches I've ever eaten in the wilderness was from a small shop in Three Rivers, California, right outside of Sequoia National Park. We grabbed sandwiches from the Three Rivers shop for a day trip up to the Kaweah River to swim, soak, and picnic. My sandwich came with a jalapeño almond pesto that was incredible.

Our version of the pesto has a little extra zing from the cilantro and lemon, and you'll find the taste infuses more and more into the other ingredients the longer the sandwich stays "pressed" in your backpack. —*Emily*

AT HOME

In the bowl of a food processor fitted with the metal blade attachment, place almonds, cilantro, jalapeño, garlic, lime juice, salt, and pepper. Process until all the ingredients are broken down into a paste, stopping to scrape down the sides as needed.

With the food processor running, drizzle in the olive oil, and process until combined.

Transfer to an airtight container and keep chilled until your trip.

Caramelized Onion Spread

Yield: About 2 cups
Prep Time: 10 minutes
Cook Time: About 1 hour

1/3 cup extra-virgin olive oil

2 pounds yellow onions, peeled and thinly sliced

1 tablespoon sugar

1/2 cup vegetable broth

2 tablespoons cider vinegar

1/2 teaspoon kosher salt

1/2 teaspoon freshly ground black pepper

Salt and pepper, to taste

My husband, Wes, worked in the food-service industry for a long time before making the transition to college professor. I enlist his help whenever possible, since he now has a dream work schedule (about fifteen hours a week, Monday through Thursday), and gets outdoors a lot as well. When I asked him to concoct some sort of caramelized onion spread for sandwiches, this is what he made. He learned it from the cooks he worked with at a fine Italian restaurant. We increased the heat at the end to pull a little more depth out of the vinegar and melt the onions even more. Be prepared to turn a plain old turkey and cheese sandwich into something amazing. —*Emily*

In a large heavy-bottomed pot or deep skillet, heat the oil over medium heat until it shimmers. Add the onions and spread out evenly across the pan, and cook over medium heat until the onions are translucent, about 15 minutes. Uncover the pan and sprinkle in the sugar. Continue cooking, stirring often, until the onions are brown and caramelized, about 30 minutes. Stir in the broth and vinegar and cook for about 20 minutes more, until the onions are brown and a little bit jammy. Add the salt and pepper, adding more to taste.

Transfer to an airtight container and keep chilled until your trip.

Roasted Red Pepper Quinoa Cakes

Yield: 6 servings

Prep Time: 20 minutes

Cook Time: 35 minutes

½ cup quinoa

1 tablespoon extra-virgin olive oil

1 cup mushrooms, finely chopped

½ cup finely chopped shallots

1 teaspoon balsamic vinegar

1 cup shredded Parmesan cheese

½ cup roasted red peppers, finely chopped

¼ cup dried bread crumbs

½ teaspoon kosher salt

½ teaspoon freshly ground black pepper

Some people like to go deep into something and get really good at it, but I'm more of a Jane of all trades type. After years of cycling and rock climbing, my latest project is SCUBA diving. The sensation of floating underwater and the excitement that comes with spotting strange and new sea creatures is surprisingly addictive. In between dives, when we are resting on the boat, it's prime snack time.

On an excursion to Catalina Island I took with my partner, Daniel, a giant sea bass sighting really worked up our appetites, but luckily we had these quinoa cakes on hand. The outside is a bit crunchy, and the Parmesan cheese brings the saltiness that one craves after exertion. A couple of these usually hit the spot and will keep you going until your next break. —*Mai-Yan*

Preheat the oven to 350°F.

Lightly grease a standard 6-cup muffin tin, and set aside.

In a medium pot, combine 1 cup water and the quinoa and bring to a boil. Reduce heat to low, cover the pot, and simmer until water has absorbed, about 15 minutes. Transfer into a large bowl and set aside.

Meanwhile, heat the olive oil in a skillet over medium heat. Sauté the mushrooms and shallots until they start to caramelize, about 15 minutes. Remove from heat. Drizzle with the balsamic vinegar, and stir.

After the quinoa has cooled slightly, stir in the cheese, red pepper, and bread crumbs. Season with salt and pepper. Mix well to combine.

Divide mixture into the 6 muffin tins, making sure each is packed tightly, and bake for about 20 minutes, until just starting to brown on top. Cool completely.

Store quinoa cakes in an airtight container and keep chilled until your trip.

Barbeque Pie Bombs

Yield: 6 pie bombs

Prep Time: 25 minutes

Cook Time: 30 to 40 minutes

1 tablespoon vegetable oil

2 (7 ounces total) Italian sausage links, halved lengthwise and chopped

½ onion, chopped

½ red bell pepper, chopped

½ cup barbeque sauce

1 piecrust, ready-made, defrosted

Aimee, Emily, and I take our birthdays seriously. Every year we plan something for each other, and the birthday girl gets to make specific requests. The best part is that it forces us to block out time to go on adventures. After years of ambitious ideas, we learned to keep it simple and focus more on the quality together time—a good rule of thumb for any outdoor adventure. A couple years ago, on a lovely birthday backpacking trip to Mount Pinos just outside Los Angeles, I took the lead for lunch on the trail with a very loose idea of a "hand pie" with a filling of sweet potatoes, leeks, jalapeños, sausage, and goat cheese. This recipe is a variation of the original version, but you can use anything you like for the filling—even leftovers—as long as the consistency is not too liquid and the ingredients can hold up unrefrigerated for at least half a day. Daniel came up with the name and likes Barbeque Pie Bombs so much that he requests them every time we go hiking. —*Mai-Yan*

This recipe calls for piecrust. If you're using a frozen piecrust, make sure it is just defrosted—slightly chilled makes it easier to handle. If you're making piecrust from scratch, you'll need to rely on your own proven method. Just be sure it's prepped in advance and chilled in the refrigerator for about an hour before you begin making these.

Preheat the oven to 350°F.

Generously coat a standard 6-cup muffin tin with cooking spray, and set aside.

Heat the oil in a skillet over medium-high heat. Add the sausage and onion, and cook for 10 minutes, stirring occasionally. Add the bell pepper, and cook for another 5 minutes. Stir in the barbeque sauce and mix well to coat all the ingredients. Remove skillet from heat and set aside.

Lightly flour a clean surface, and form the piecrust into a ball. Evenly divide the dough into six pieces. Using a lightly floured rolling pin, roll out each piece to form a 6- to 7-inch circle.

Place one dough circle into each of the muffin tins, making sure not to poke holes in the dough as you lightly press it down into the shape. You should have enough extra dough hanging over the edges that the dough will reach the middle point of the pie when folded. Fill each with 3 tablespoons of filling. The filling should reach the top edge of the muffin tin.

Gently fold one side of the dough toward the center of the filling. (Don't pull the dough as it probably is getting soft at this point and is vulnerable to tearing.) Create a pleat by pinching the left hand part of the half circle that is already touching the dough. Take the pleat and fold it toward the center of the pie. Repeat this step going clockwise, until the filling is enclosed in the dough. Repeat this step for each pie.

Bake the pies for 30 to 40 minutes or until the dough is golden brown and flaky. Use a butter knife to gently dislodge the pies from the tin. Let cool, then wrap in foil or in pack in an airtight container to take with you. Keep chilled until you leave for your trip.

CAR CAMPING

Car camping is a part of every adventurer's life. Some of us conjure nothing else when we think about being in the great outdoors, while others use this type of camping as a base to move deeper into the wild. You can be as minimalist or glamorous as you like, and choose to camp with a large group, your family, or just your closest friend.

BASICS

Think of car camping recipes as slight variations of favorite home-cooked meals. A simple camp stove or a campfire is all you need to start, and you usually have the luxury of a cooler for perishables.

Sometimes it can feel like car camping requires a huge setup to be happy, but this isn't true! Start out with the basic gear, and add only what you really missed the last time. As you gain more outdoor experience, you will get a better sense of your true needs and therefore what is actually essential for *you* to enjoy the outdoors.

We've compiled a list of essentials for any car camping trip—our Car Camping Base Kit. These are items that should come with you every time. They also happen to be things that are most easily forgotten—the staples rarely thought about since they are always around at home. Keep the list handy or, better yet, keep a camping bin stocked with the items, ready to go. From here, add on any specific items needed for the recipes you plan to cook or the specific campsite you are heading out to enjoy. For example, a water jug may be important if your campsite doesn't have potable water available. A two-burner stove and, of course, pots and pans, will end up in your camping toolbox on most occasions. If you choose a menu of all campfire recipes, however, you may choose to bring only a Dutch oven instead.

Even with all of our checklists we've found ourselves in plenty of situations without the exact tool needed. This is bound to happen to you too, so plan to get creative and improvise if necessary.

CAR CAMPING BASE KIT

"Car Camping Base Kit" is included as one "tool" in each car camping recipe, and any extra items specific to the recipe will be listed in addition to this. This list is also provided as a checklist in the Appendix. We've also included a list of our favorite car camping extras. We find these make a big impact on comfort and happiness, so we include them on all of our journeys.

- ☐ Aluminum foil
- ☐ Bottle opener
- ☐ Can opener
- ☐ Chef's knife
- ☐ Cooking spray/oil
- ☐ Cooler
- ☐ Cutting board
- ☐ Dish towel
- ☐ Dishwashing tub
- ☐ Gallon ziplock bags
- ☐ Long tongs
- ☐ Matches/lighter
- ☐ Measuring cups and spoons, or multiuse items such as a water bottle or stirring spoon with measurements already notated
- ☐ Paper towels
- ☐ Plates, bowls, utensils, drinkware
- ☐ Salt and pepper
- ☐ Spatula
- ☐ Sponge and biodegradable soap
- ☐ Trash bags
- ☐ Wooden mixing spoon

CAR CAMPING NICETIES

- ☐ Assorted jars for ingredients and/or leftovers
- ☐ Collapsible, unbreakable vase
- ☐ Enamelware everything
- ☐ Lanterns, preferably solar powered
- ☐ LED tea light candles
- ☐ Oversized cloth napkins and/or bandanas
- ☐ Tablecloth
- ☐ Wool blankets for the backs of chairs and picnics

ORGANIZING YOUR CAR CAMPING KITCHEN

Organizing your kitchen-away-from-home can seem simple upon arrival to camp, but the kitchen area gets chaotic with impressive speed! *Starting out* your trip with a system is the only way to control it. First, get all the kitchen food and gear to the picnic table. Set up any extra tables and

Jars with tight-fitting lids are a campsite's great multitasker: storage, transport, and prep. Use them for smaller amounts of pantry staples or to separate leftovers for guests at the end of the trip. You can also use them to emulsify salad dressing, scramble eggs, or whip cream! They aren't included in the base kit tools, because you can choose from multiple sizes and quantities for each adventure, but we do recommend them.

designate a parking spot for gear and food bins, preferably not on tables. Reorganize coolers and bins by drinks, snack food, and ingredients and label them to keep people from snacking on the cheese that was assigned to Foil Packet Nachos, for instance.

We recommend storing dry goods in tough lidded bins, keeping the lids on most of the day for weather- and critter-proofing.

Your kitchen should be far from the sleeping area but close to the campfire and hangout space. This makes people, like Aimee's mom, happy when they sneak off to bed early. It also prevents any critters from looking for (and finding!) crumbs around your tent.

MEAL PLANNING

Planning is the most helpful thing you can do for yourself before a camping trip. Keep these tips in mind when you're in that phase of the process.

Assign a "host" if you're camping with multiple families. The host (probably you, since you're reading this cookbook) should be responsible for bringing the main ingredients for the main meals, as well as essentials like the Car Camping Base Kit, firewood, and ice. Delegate items like drinks and appetizers that are easier to live without if someone forgets or decides not to come.

Plan, plan, plan. Where are you going? Who are you feeding? Will there be water? Will there be bear lockers? What is the weather going to be like? What activities will you be doing? How many people are you cooking for? What recipes will you be making and when? The more questions you can even *estimate* answers to before you go, the easier it will be to deal with the inevitable surprises.

Measure out all possible ingredients before leaving home. It is much easier to divvy up a can of beans and leave half at home in your fridge than it is to keep the unused portion in your cooler. It's also helpful to label containers of prepped ingredients with the recipe name so you know what's what when you get to camp. Whenever possible, our recipes utilize whole amounts of items. For instance, a recipe will call for "1 onion" as opposed to "1 cup of chopped onions," and if canned beans are used, the recipe will incorporate the juice from the can.

Plan for portions, but be prepared for leftovers anyway. It's easy to fear not having enough food, especially when you can't just run down to the market. This encourages overpacking. Try to be realistic about how much of a dish you really need to make for your group, taking into consideration the activity level to assess how hungry people may be at the end of the day. Just be sure to have containers with lids or at least ziplock bags to store any leftovers to reduce waste. In many cases, you won't have a great option for disposing of trash, and may even have to pack it out with you. Please avoid dumping food in the fire unless you know it will burn down fully. Woodland creatures *will* walk across hot coals for a corncob.

Get creative with tomorrow's recipes. If you properly save leftovers, they can be a great addition to breakfast or lunch the next day. Too much chili for dinner? Slap it onto hamburgers the next day. Leftover fondue makes an impressive grilled cheese sandwich. Or add extra veggies to the next pasta meal.

CAMPFIRE COOKING

A two-burner stove is the go-to tool for most car camping recipes, but learning to cook over the campfire opens up a great deal of possibilities. It's also a fun way to experience a type of cooking more unique to car camping. There are other benefits too: a campfire makes cooking a more inclusive activity, keeping the cook near the warmth, conversation, and potential helpers. And it is also a form of cooking that whispers about survival, allowing you to build a deeper connection with the wilderness.

Dutch oven cooking is the most technical way to use a fire, and you will find tips here on how to figure out temperature and make some impressively complex recipes under the stars. This book is about *camp* cooking rather than Dutch oven mastery, though, so we are generally a little loose in our expectations of exact temperatures and even heating. The campfire is there for enjoyment and warmth, as well as cooking, so we guesstimate how many coals pulled from the fire are equal to the amount of uniform charcoal briquettes calculated by our Dutch Oven Baking Charcoal Chart (see Appendix). We prefer to feel our way through the process and to stand behind our "rustic" burned edges. Camping is about letting go of the stresses of normal lives, so campfire cooking should follow suit.

HOW TO BUILD A CAMPFIRE

There are many ways to build a campfire. Most people subscribe to the method that involves throwing sticks and paper and lighter fluid into a pile in no particular order, and continuing to light matches until something eventually holds a flame. This method eventually works, but it is not efficient, and it is not the best option when a cooking timeframe is involved.

Some people do a more formal job of setting up their stick, paper, and lighter fluid combination into a beautiful, if rickety tipi construction. Unfortunately, once the tipi starts burning, it crumbles into a disheveled pile that loses its necessary air column and needs to be worked to come back to life again.

Over the years, we perfected our version of a log cabin fire. If you spend the time to build a log cabin out of kindling in the beginning, you should be able to easily light a tinder nest that catches the kindling with only one match. The kindling will not fall and impede the air column in the center as easily as in other methods, so you'll have more time to add fuel logs to build up your bed of coals.

The key is to spend time setting up your structure *before* lighting it and having back stock of kindling nearby just in case. Remember to use only downed wood or wood purchased from the local camp store or host.

There are three components in a good campfire structure.

1. **Tinder:** Build a "tinder nest" with whatever you can find, including dry pine needles, cardboard, paper towels, and tiny sticks. The tinder should light on fire with ease, but it won't hold a flame for very long. Its purpose is to light the kindling.

2. **Kindling:** Kindling is made up of thin sticks that light a little less easily than tinder, but once lit, they hold onto the flame and heat for longer. This category ranges in thickness from the size of a pencil to larger shards of a fuel log. The smaller of these pieces are placed toward the bottom. Stack kindling into the shape of a log cabin around the tinder nest.

3. **Fuel:** Time for the big logs! Any type of wood works as fuel as long as it has been dried out (seasoned) sufficiently. Soft wood catches more quickly than hard wood and so builds embers faster. As a result, soft wood won't last as long so you'll need more of it. Hard wood takes longer to start, but produces better coals and less smoke, so it's worth the wait for a cooking fire.

CAMPFIRE COOKING TOOLS

There are a lot of tools that will make campfire cooking more interesting and fun, but none of them are technically "essential." If you have been practicing to go on *Survivor*, like Emily's husband, you probably can cook on a fire using tools found in the wilderness. For the rest of us, we offer a list of our favorite campfire cooking items. Unlike the Car Camping Base Kit, these will be listed individually in the "Tools" list when needed for a recipe.

- Cast iron skillet
- Dutch oven with lid lifter
- Hatchet
- Heatproof gloves
- Lid stand
- Non-plastic cooking utensils, such as a metal spatula
- Pie iron

COOKING ON THE GRATE

If your campsite has a fire ring, it likely includes a grate that can be placed over the fire pit as well. The grate can be used much like a stovetop, and heat can be adjusted by manipulating the campfire underneath. Add wood directly under your food to turn up the heat, or scoop it away to the other side of the fire pit to cool things down. You can use the campfire grate for anything from grilling meat and vegetables to heating a big pot of beans or stew.

COOKING WITH AN ALUMINUM FOIL POUCH

If you don't own any cast iron or cookware that can get sooty, you can make an aluminum foil pouch to cook food instead. Foil pouches can go on the grate or in the fire. Food will cook more quickly and stick more easily, but this is a great way to concentrate the flavors of a sauce or marinade, and you can just toss the foil in the trash after you're finished. See the Appendix for directions on how to make an aluminum foil pouch.

COFFEE AND CAMPING

What is the best way to make coffee? It's an age-old question, but rather than getting closer to a universal answer, there is instead an increase in *possible* answers. We have put every method to the test, from percolators to pour overs, and still haven't come to a decisive conclusion.

The question of how to make coffee in the wilderness has just as many answers. To save you time, here's our full rundown of options tried and loved. We can all agree that coffee is a very personal matter, so you may have to try a couple ways until you find your perfect cup of joe. Whichever method you land on as "the one," please do not leave grounds in the backcountry (even if you bury them). This is a Leave No Trace no-no.

Aeropress: Aeropress is the best method if you like espresso and a lightweight setup. There are less grounds overall because the beans are stronger and finer ground, but it does require a filter, adding to your waste. The press weighs less than 8 ounces but it includes multiple parts that can be lost or forgotten. It takes a few rounds to make enough coffee for a crowd, but people will think you're fancy!

Cold brew: If you want minimal effort in the morning, make your coffee the night before as a cold brew. We make it in a spare water bottle in concentrate form. By volume, combine one part coarsely ground coffee with eight parts water, and let steep overnight. The next morning strain the coffee through cheesecloth, making sure to pack out your grounds. We call it "moon-brewed coffee." You can drink it cold, or heat some water and make an Americano.

Cowboy coffee: Cowboy coffee is coffee making in its most minimal form. Boil some water in a pot and add coffee grounds directly to the water. Drip a few drops of cold water on top to get the grounds to start sinking. Then remove from heat and wrap the pot in a down jacket to keep it hot while the coffee finishes steeping. If done correctly, you should be able to pour grounds-free coffee into your cup, with grounds remaining at the bottom of the pot. There are other ways to make cowboy coffee, but we prefer this one, taught to us by our friend Adan.

Instant: There are some pretty good options for instant coffee nowadays, but other types still outcompete instant for quality. This is the simplest method: heat water, pour a single serving of instant coffee into your mug, and then add the hot water, allowing it to swirl and dissolve easily. Stir it up a little more if needed to dissolve the freeze-dried or ultrafine grounds, leaving you with no coffee grounds to cleanup.

Pour-over: A pour-over is a good option if you need to make just one cup at a time, and it can also be very lightweight (although there are options for whole carafes of pour-over coffee if desired). It requires a filter that needs to be disposed of, but this type of filter holds the leftover grounds, which keeps things tidy. You can easily add flavorings, like cinnamon, to a pour-over coffee, which is a perk if you're looking for a gourmet option.

Press pot: A press pot, also known as a French press, is good for making larger amounts of coffee. The flavor of coffee from a press pot differs from filtered options because the oils don't get filtered out. Some presses are insulated, and can double as carafes, keeping the extra coffee warm while you drink leisurely at camp. Some cooksets and stoves on the market can be fit with a press accessory, keeping you from having to bring along a one-use tool. If you plan to make coffee in the same pot you used to make dinner the night before, however, beware of the possibility of leftover flavors and clean the pot well between uses.

COOKING WITH CAST IRON

Cast iron is our preferred material for campfire cooking vessels. It is inexpensive, durable, and even-heating. Cast iron campfire cooking lets you cook with very high heat—the ideal way to get crispy and crunchy textures into your food. If properly cared for, it is naturally nonstick and requires only a little hot water and some scraping to clean up. Cast iron has the ability to hold in heat for longer than other materials, so it works well for serving things directly from the pan, whether still on the grate or moved to a table.

Cast iron is heavy, but it is generally used only when you're car camping, so weight isn't an issue. To keep Dutch oven meals warm, throw a few coals into a cast iron skillet and put the Dutch oven on top. This setup can sit through a whole meal at the table. If you plan to do backcountry campfire cooking—and don't have a pack animal to carry your Dutch oven—consider cooking over a grate or in a foil pouch instead.

PIE IRON COOKING

One of our favorite cast iron tools is the pie iron. We originally thought of it as a one-use-wonder sort of tool—the type of tool we tend to avoid—but after experimenting with it, we realized how versatile it is.

A pie iron is basically a cast iron sandwich press. It is made up of two pieces of cast iron on sticks that press together and can be handheld over the fire. There are multiple shapes and sizes available, meant for different purposes. We gravitate toward the sandwich-style versions, because they are the most versatile, but pie irons also come in waffle shapes and hot dog shapes, and deeper configurations that are good for cakes and frittatas.

Pie irons are inexpensive so we recommend acquiring several of them to allow multiple people to cook up their own favorite concoctions simultaneously. Several of our favorite pie iron recipes are included in this chapter, but even without a pie iron, you can make many of these recipes in a skillet. If you don't have a campfire but still want to use your pie iron, you can use them over the flame of a gas stove (at camp or at home).

Pie irons can transform leftovers. One of our favorite recipes is the pie iron spaghetti melt, made from leftover spaghetti from the night before. Sandwich spaghetti and a slice of mozzarella cheese between two pieces of garlic bread. Lunch will be ready in minutes and it will taste just like baked pasta straight out of the oven.

DUTCH OVEN COOKING

There are many types of Dutch ovens, all with slightly varied purposes. Crock style Dutch ovens with flat bottoms and domed lids are meant for cooking on a stovetop or a campfire grate or in a home oven. These work well for cooking a stew or curry that only needs to be heated from the bottom rather than truly baked.

The Dutch ovens we generally use to bake in the campfire are made for using with coals. They have legs that raise the oven up and a flanged lid for holding coals. They also have a wire handle to make it easy to pull the oven out of the fire. We occasionally use this type of Dutch oven on the grate but it takes a bit of finagling to get the feet to sit properly.

As mentioned before, you can get precise with temperatures if you're using uniform charcoal briquettes. Many expert Dutch-oven cooks use heatproof tables and charcoal to do their baking. Campfires create nice coals for you if you're patient, but if you want to keep the fire going for warmth while you are cooking, you'll need to do a bit more cooking management since the Dutch oven will sit next to the fire, causing one side to heat faster than the other. When you have a nice bed of coals, scoot the burning logs to one side of your pit, ideally on the side that you can put the grate over, in case you need to cook on the grate at the same time. This will leave the other side open to add back as many coals as you need for your Dutch oven recipe.

The main thing to remember with Dutch-oven cooking is that heat rises. This means it actually takes about two-thirds more heat *on top* of the oven than underneath to get the vessel to heat evenly. This is most important when baking.

Start by looking up your desired temperature using our Dutch Oven Baking Chart (see the Appendix). A typical charcoal briquette is roughly two inches by two inches and one inch thick. It's likely you will have pieces that are larger or smaller than a typical briquette when using hot coals from your campfire. But don't worry too much about getting exact counts! Remember, improvisation is a big part of camp cooking, so have some fun with it.

Have a look at the lump coal pieces in your fire. Smaller ones are best left underneath your oven so that it doesn't get high-centered or tilted. Use a pair of long tongs to move larger pieces on top of the lid. They hold their heat longer than the small ones, reducing ash build-up, which cools things down and can get into the food.

If you have a fire going on the side, remember to rotate your oven every fifteen minutes or so. Since there are two separate heat sources (coals under the oven and on the lid), it's important to rotate the whole oven and the lid independently of each other. A general rule of thumb is to turn the whole oven a half turn in one direction, and the lid a quarter turn in the other to keep the heat evenly distributed.

RECIPES

BREAKFAST

APPETIZERS

SIDE DISHES

ENTREES

DRINKS

DESSERTS

BREAKFASTS

Chilaquiles

Yield: 4 servings
Prep Time: 2 minutes
Cook Time: 5 minutes

6 eggs
1 tablespoon oil or cooking spray
3 cups of your favorite salsa
About 30 tortilla chips (6 ounces)
1 cup crumbled queso fresco

FOR SERVING

Sour cream
Avocado
Chopped cilantro

TOOLS

Car Camping Base Kit
10-inch cast iron skillet
Heatproof gloves

I make these chilaquiles, a popular Mexican breakfast dish, on special mornings at home. I've experimented making them many different ways and love to survey my friends about their favorite methods. But the simplest is my favorite, and it's definitely the easiest to prep on a morning at camp. Five ingredients, one skillet, and about fifteen minutes is all you need. You don't even need plates. I love queso fresco here, but if you can't find it, use shredded sharp cheddar in its place. —*Emily*

AT HOME

Crack the eggs into a Mason jar with a tight-fitting lid. This makes for easy transport in your cooler.

AT CAMP

Preheat the cast iron skillet on the stovetop over medium-high heat. Coat it with oil or cooking spray.

Scramble the eggs by shaking the jar. (This is a good kid job.)

Pour the chips into the skillet, and then immediately add the egg over the top, stirring occasionally to begin scrambling them and coat the chips. Add the salsa, and continue stirring to coat. Once the salsa is heated through, about 2 minutes, remove skillet from the heat and sprinkle the mixture with the cheese.

Serve immediately with sour cream, avocado, and cilantro.

Hot Chocolate Oatmeal

Yield: 2 servings
Prep Time: 5 minutes
Cook Time: 10 minutes

2¼ cups water or milk
¼ cup hot cocoa mix
1 cup rolled oats
Pinch of kosher salt

FOR SERVING (OPTIONAL)

Whipped cream
Marshmallows
Crumbled chocolate bar
Sprinkles

TOOLS

Car Camping Base Kit
Medium pot

Oatmeal makes for a convenient and quick camp breakfast that fuels the body better than anything else. So we continue to create new versions of the stuff. This is a sweet one and is as convenient as the regular old version. In fact, it may even one-up the convenience of plain oatmeal if you're the type to drink hot cocoa with your meal. This is yummy and only requires one vessel to consume and to clean. This recipe is written for two servings, but is easily doubled or tripled for a group. Serve it with whipped cream, marshmallows, and chocolate sprinkles, of course, which you should already have packed for s'mores anyway. —*Emily*

In a medium pot over high heat, bring the water or milk to a boil. Add the hot cocoa mix, and stir to combine. Add the oatmeal and salt, and stir to combine. Reduce the heat to low and simmer until the oatmeal is to your desired consistency, about 5 minutes.

Divide the mixture into two bowls. Add your chosen toppings.

Peanut Butter and Jelly Overnight Oats

Yield: 1 serving

Prep Time: 5 minutes

²/₃ cup unsweetened almond milk (other types of milk work too)

½ cup rolled oats

2 tablespoons salted natural peanut butter

1 tablespoon chia seeds (optional)

1 to 2 tablespoons jam of choice

FOR SERVING

Sliced bananas, berries, or other fruit

TOOLS

Car Camping Base Kit

2-cup Mason jar with lid

My parents took my brother and me camping all the time when we were growing up. My mom says it was the one thing they could do with us that was affordable, kept us entertained, and made them both happy. As a parent of twins, Asha and Ravi, who are now five, I've learned how true this really is. We camp as often as we can, usually last-minute overnighters to escape our to-do lists in exchange for some quality family time. On these types of trips, I try to keep the food as simple as possible so that we can focus on just getting out the door.

Peanut Butter and Jelly Overnight Oats are a camp breakfast staple for those mornings when we want to get up and go. You can make them at home the night before your trip, or while you're making dinner at camp, then throw the Mason jars in the cooler. Come morning, there's no need to pull out stoves or do dishes—just go play! —*Aimee*

The evening before you want to eat this, prepare the oats. In a Mason jar, combine milk, oats, peanut butter, and seeds. Stir to combine, but don't worry about getting the peanut butter perfectly mixed in. Top the oatmeal with a tablespoon or two of jam (depending on how sweet you like it). Seal the jar with a lid, and place in a cooler overnight.

In the morning, serve the oatmeal cold, topped with fruit.

Variation: Marmalade and Mocha Almond Butter

Substitute Mocha Almond Butter (see On the Trail Recipes, Sweet Snacks) for the peanut butter, and use orange marmalade for the jam. Top with toasted chopped almonds.

PEANUT BUTTER AND JELLY OVERNIGHT OATS (PG 75)

CROQUE MADAMES

Croque Madames

Yield: 2 sandwiches

Prep Time: 5 minutes

Cook Time: 15 minutes

3/4 teaspoon Dijon mustard

4 slices sourdough bread

4 slices of Gruyere cheese

4 to 8 slices of Black Forest ham

2 eggs

Spray oil

Pinch of kosher salt and freshly ground black pepper

TOOLS

Car Camping Base Kit

Nonstick skillet, any size

This recipe is easy but impressive. Your friends will think you're fancy, even if you aren't because the *Frenchness* of the ingredients makes the recipe feel sophisticated. Really it's a grilled cheese with a toad in a hole. *Pas mal, non*? To keep things simple, we replaced the intimidating béchamel sauce with a good schmear of zingy Dijon. That's French too, by the way. *Bon appétit*! —Mai-Yan

Slather two slices of bread with the mustard. Add 1 slice of cheese per slice of bread, followed by 2 to 4 slices of ham on top of each. Set aside.

Lay out the remaining two slices of bread on a hard surface. Using a knife or circular object that is smaller than the size of the bread, cut out a hole in the center. The holed bread slices are for the top of your sandwiches. (Toast up the bread hole as well, and use it to sop up any leftover fried egg, cheese, or mustard at the end.)

Heat the skillet on medium heat, then spray with oil. Lay holed bread down and occasionally press down with a spatula until bread is crispy and golden brown, about 3 minutes. Flip the bread and crack one egg into each hole. Sprinkle egg with a pinch of salt and pepper. (Keep the heat at medium so that egg cooks but the bread doesn't burn.) When most of the egg white is cooked, gently flip the bread slices again and cook for another 5 minutes. (Note: If you want a sunny-side-up egg, do not flip the bread and keep cooking until your egg white is cooked through.)

Place the grilled bread with egg on top of the ham and cheese sandwich half, and put the assembled sandwich back into the skillet, non-egg-side down. Grill the sandwich on medium heat until the cheese is melted. Serve immediately.

Skillet Frittata

Yield: 4 to 6 servings
Prep Time: 10 minutes
Cook Time: 30 minutes

1 medium onion, diced

1 bell pepper, diced

1 cup mushrooms, diced

1 cup fresh spinach, chopped

8 eggs

1 cup shredded Parmesan cheese, divided

$\frac{1}{2}$ teaspoon kosher salt

$\frac{1}{2}$ teaspoon freshly ground black pepper

1 tablespoon extra-virgin olive oil

TOOLS

Car Camping Base Kit
10- or 12-inch cast iron skillet with lid
Heatproof gloves

We often camp with a pretty large group, everyone with an individual morning routine. So rather than try to sit down to breakfast at once, we rely on recipes like this Skillet Frittata. Frittatas are usually baked, but this stovetop skillet option doesn't require a morning campfire. Using cast iron keeps it from burning on the bottom too easily while cooking, and allows it to stay warm until early risers return from morning hikes and meditations or the late sleepers crawl out of their tents. It can also be eaten at room temperature for those who *still* aren't ready for breakfast when the masses return (but they better hide a piece or it'll likely be gone). —*Mai-Yan*

AT HOME

Prepare all of the vegetables. Dice the onion, bell pepper, and mushrooms. Chop the spinach. Store in separate containers.

Crack all the eggs into a quart-sized Mason jar.

AT CAMP

Into the jar of eggs, add $\frac{1}{2}$ cup of the cheese, salt, and pepper, and close the lid. Shake the jar to beat the eggs. Set aside.

Heat the oil in a skillet over medium-high heat. Add the onion and sauté until softened, about 5 minutes. Add the bell pepper and mushroom. Sauté until tender, another 5 minutes. Add the spinach, and stir to just slightly wilt.

Pour the egg mixture over the vegetables, and mix well. Reduce the heat to low and cover with a lid. Cook until the eggs are solid, about 20 minutes.

When the eggs are cooked through, sprinkle the remaining $\frac{1}{2}$ cup of cheese on top of the egg mixture, and cover again to melt, about 2 minutes.

Serve warm, or cool to room temperature if desired, slicing into wedges.

English Muffins with Strawberry Skillet Jam

Yield: 8 muffins and about 1½ cups of jam

Prep Time: 20 minutes plus 1½ hours rising time

Cook Time: 25 minutes

FOR THE ENGLISH MUFFINS

3 cups bread flour, plus more for rolling

1 tablespoon sugar

1¼ teaspoons instant yeast

¾ teaspoon kosher salt

⅔ cup milk

⅔ cup water

2 tablespoons butter

2 tablespoons cornmeal

Cooking spray

Not many people think to make English muffins from scratch, but they're surprisingly easy and they don't require an oven. You also don't have to knead the dough! For convenience, make the dough the night before; the longer they rise, the more flavorful the dough. But if time does not permit, you can still make the dough in the morning. The Strawberry Skillet Jam is thickened with chia seeds so it comes together quickly while the muffins are cooking. If you want something savory, skip the jam and make fried egg sandwiches instead. —Aimee

AT HOME

In a large ziplock bag (or bowl with a lid), combine the flour, sugar, yeast, and salt.

AT CAMP

In a small pot over low heat, warm the milk, water, and butter until the butter is melted. Transfer mixture to a large bowl. Cool until it's lukewarm.

FOR THE JAM

2 cups sliced strawberries

2 to 4 tablespoons sugar

Juice of 1 small lemon

1 tablespoon chia seeds

1 pinch of kosher salt

FOR SERVING

Butter

TOOLS

Car Camping Base Kit

Small pot

Large mixing bowl

Plastic wrap or a tea towel

Parchment paper and tape or a silicone baking mat

Rolling pin, clean water or wine bottle

Biscuit cutter or drinking glass

Large cast iron skillet or a medium pot

Griddle or additional large cast iron skillet

Heatproof gloves

Add the flour and yeast mixture to milk mixture, and stir well to combine, making a soft dough. Cover the mixture with plastic wrap or a lid, and let rise either overnight in your cooler or for about an hour in a warm place, until the dough is nearly doubled in size.

Transfer the dough to a clean work surface and dust it with flour. (A silicone baking mat works well, or tape some parchment paper to a camp table.) Roll out the dough to about ½ inch thick. With a biscuit cutter or drinking glass, cut rounds and set them aside onto your work surface. Sprinkle the tops and bottoms of the rounds with cornmeal and cover them with a clean towel. Let rise for about 30 minutes.

While the dough is rising, make the jam. In a large cast iron skillet or a medium pot set over medium heat, place the berries and sugar. Mash the berries with a wooden spoon or a fork, until the berries soften and release their juices, about 5 minutes. Stir in the lemon juice, chia seeds, and salt. Remove from heat and let stand until the muffins are done.

Once the muffins have risen, grease a griddle and heat over medium heat. Cook the muffins on the griddle for about 5 minutes per side, or until they're lightly browned and cooked through.

Split the muffins and serve warm with butter and jam.

Blueberry Baked Oatmeal

Yield: 6 servings

Prep Time: 10 minutes

Cook Time: 20 to 25 minutes

2 cups rolled oats

3 tablespoons brown sugar

1 teaspoon cinnamon

1 teaspoon baking powder

1/2 teaspoon kosher salt

3 tablespoons butter

2 cups blueberries, divided

2 cups milk

2 eggs (or 2 tablespoons ground flax plus 6 tablespoons water)

1/2 cup applesauce

1 tablespoon vanilla extract

FOR SERVING

Maple syrup

Milk

TOOLS

Car Camping Base Kit

10-inch Dutch oven

Medium mixing bowl

Whisk

Lid lifter

Heatproof gloves

I know this isn't the dessert section of the book, but I need to let you in on a secret—Blueberry Baked Oatmeal is pretty much breakfast bread pudding: it's warm, comforting, soft, and just the right amount of sweet and tart to help keep it in the breakfast realm. It *is* oatmeal, but like no oatmeal you've ever tasted. And if you don't want to bring eggs (or you forget them), substitute with 1 tablespoon flax mixed with 3 tablespoons water per egg instead.

We tested this recipe on a camping trip to Carrizo Plain National Monument, and despite our "failed" first attempt, our Dutch oven was scraped clean by our professional taste-testers. The surrounding California poppies, popcorn flowers, and rancher's fiddleheads exploding with color probably helped! We present this as a large portion so you can share the love and feed all your friends and family with it. —*Mai-Yan*

AT HOME

In a large ziplock bag, combine the oats, brown sugar, cinnamon, baking powder, and salt.

AT CAMP

Place the Dutch oven on a grate set over a campfire. Add the butter, melting it completely.

In a medium bowl, carefully pour the melted butter, leaving a little behind to keep the Dutch oven oiled.

Add 1 cup of the blueberries to the Dutch oven. Make sure the oat mixture is well combined, then pour it on top of the berries.

To the butter bowl, add the milk, eggs, applesauce, and vanilla. Whisk to combine, then pour on top of the oats. Submerge any oats that didn't get covered in liquid, then scatter the remaining cup of blueberries on top. Cover the Dutch oven.

Adjust your fire so that you have room to place the entire Dutch oven next to the fire on a level surface with very few to no coals

underneath it. Place the oven next to a medium fire and add about 14 coals on the lid. Let it bake for 10 minutes, and then take a peek to make sure nothing is burning.

Rotate the oven 180 degrees so the other half is facing the fire. Also, rotate the lid one-quarter turn in the opposite direction of the Dutch oven body to redistribute heat from the lid. (If your fire is getting too hot, move the Dutch oven farther away from the flame to avoid burning the sides of the oatmeal.) Let it bake for another 10 minutes, and take a look. The top should be golden brown and the oatmeal thickened with a little moisture remaining. If there is still a lot of liquid, repeat the Dutch oven body and lid rotation (as above) and let it bake for another 5 minutes.

Serve hot with a little maple syrup and milk, if desired.

Veggie Tofu Scramble

Yield: 4 servings

Prep Time: 10 minutes

Cook Time: 20 minutes

1 bell pepper, diced

½ onion, diced

1 cup mushrooms, diced

1 cup kale, chopped

1 tablespoon extra-virgin olive oil

1 (14-ounce) block firm tofu

½ teaspoon turmeric

½ teaspoon kosher salt

½ teaspoon freshly ground black pepper

1 cup shredded cheddar cheese (or vegan alternative)

TOOLS

Car Camping Base Kit

10-inch skillet with lid

Wes has been vegan for about twenty years. When I met him, several members of our extended family were working through different levels of vegetarianism, practicing how to reduce or eliminate dairy and eggs with delicious and effective substitutes. Those who haven't made the transition are now more open-minded about eating meals that are free of animal products, and it is nice for all of us to exist in an environment where food opinions are not always at the center of conversation. This recipe is one of the original Wes contributions, and if he's on the camping trip, he's sure to be whipping it up in the morning. It's a pretty simple recipe, and mimics a frittata or omelet. We add a bit of turmeric to color the tofu so the egg eaters don't even flinch.

Many car camping recipes actually dehydrate well and transition well to the backcountry. This recipe is one of them! Stick the whole thing into the oven and dry at 250°F for about three hours. It doesn't need to dry out completely, but should get to the consistency of dried fruit. Rehydrate it with two cups of water at camp, and then re-fry it again if desired. —*Emily*

AT HOME

Prepare all of the vegetables. Dice the bell pepper, onion, and mushrooms. Chop the kale. Store the onion in one container, and the rest of the vegetables in another.

AT CAMP

Heat the oil in the skillet over medium-high heat, add the onion, and sauté until softened, about 5 minutes. Add the rest of the vegetables and cook until tender, about 5 minutes more.

Drain the tofu and crumble it into the skillet on top of the vegetables. Add the turmeric, salt, and pepper, stirring to combine. Continue to cook until the tofu is heated through, about 10 minutes. Season with more salt to taste. Sprinkle the cheese across the top and cover with a lid until the cheese melts, about 3 minutes. Remove from heat and serve.

VEGGIE TOFU SCRAMBLE

PIE IRON TOASTER PASTRIES (PG 86)

Pie Iron Toaster Pastries

Yield: About 9 pastries

Prep Time: 15 minutes

Cook Time: 5 minutes per pastry

½ cup cream cheese, softened

¼ cup powdered sugar

2 sheets puff pastry, thawed

½ cup jam

Spray oil

TOOLS

Car Camping Base Kit

Small mixing bowl

Silicone baking mat, extra large cutting board, or other clean work surface

Pie iron(s)

Heatproof gloves

Toaster pastries were one of the first things I was allowed to "cook" for myself as a child. With a pie iron, they are just as easy to make at camp—even for a kid. Premade puff pastry sheets are a dream to work with at a campsite. You can fill them with pretty much anything you like and cook them quickly over the fire. This recipe calls for cream cheese and jam. Experiment with your own favorite combinations to make something your whole family will love. —Aimee

---

In a small bowl, combine the cream cheese and powdered sugar, stirring with a spoon until the mixture is relatively smooth. Set aside.

Unfold the puff pastry, and cut it into shapes to fit whatever shape pie iron you have. Spread about a tablespoon of cream cheese mixture onto half of the puff pastry pieces, and a tablespoon of jam on the remaining puff pastry pieces. Sandwich together one piece of cream cheese pastry with one piece of jam pastry, pressing the sides closed to seal. (This doesn't have to be super tight as the pie iron edges will seal it further.)

Meanwhile, preheat your pie iron over a campfire. Once the pie iron is hot, carefully open it and spray it with oil. Then place a toaster pastry inside. Close the pie iron and lock it in place. Cook the pastry over hot coals for about 5 minutes, turning often. The cooking time will greatly depend on how hot your fire is and where in the fire you're placing the pie iron, so check it often (especially the first one you cook). When the pastry is puffed up and golden brown, it's done.

Dutch Oven Sticky Buns

Yield: 8 to 10 sticky buns

Prep Time: 30 minutes, plus 1½ hours rising time

Cook Time: 15 to 25 minutes

FOR THE DOUGH

2¼ cups bread flour, plus more for rolling the dough

¼ cup sugar

1 packet (2¼ teaspoons) instant yeast

1 teaspoon kosher salt

1 cup plus 2 tablespoons milk

3 tablespoons butter

1 egg

FOR THE FILLING

⅓ cup sugar

1 tablespoon all-purpose flour

2 teaspoons cinnamon

FOR THE GLAZE

1 cup pecans

½ cup brown sugar

¼ teaspoon kosher salt

½ cup butter

¼ cup maple syrup

TOOLS

Car Camping Base Kit

Small pot

Large mixing bowl

Plastic wrap or a clean tea towel

Silicone baking mat, extra large cutting board, or other clean work surface

10-inch Dutch oven

Lid lifter

Heatproof gloves

Hot, gooey sticky buns are entirely possible when camping if you have a fire and a Dutch oven. They're made upside down, so you'll need to be extra cautious not to burn the sticky topping. Because the cast iron retains heat so well, the buns will continue cooking after you remove the Dutch oven from the fire, so make sure to pull the oven off the campfire right when the buns are barely golden brown. I admit, this recipe requires some planning and work, but it's worth it! There's nothing quite like eating home-made hot sticky buns straight out of the campfire. —*Aimee*

You can cook with your Dutch oven on the grate and coals on top if you are concerned with the temperature getting too hot underneath.

AT HOME

Prepare the dry ingredients for the dough. In a ziplock bag (or a bowl with a lid), combine the flour, sugar, yeast, and salt. Note that if you don't have *instant* yeast, you can use active dry yeast, but then don't mix it in with the flour mixture; pack it separately. Also bring about ¼ cup additional flour in a separate container.

Prepare the filling and the glaze. For the filling, combine the sugar, flour, and cinnamon in a container with a lid. For the glaze, place the pecans, brown sugar, and salt in a separate lidded container.

AT CAMP

First, make the dough. In a small pot over medium heat, heat the milk and butter until the butter is melted, about 5 minutes. Set aside until mixture cools a bit but is still warm to the touch. Lightly beat the egg with a fork and add it to the cooled milk mixture.

In a large bowl, transfer the milk mixture and add the dry dough ingredients that you prepared at home. (If you're using active dry yeast instead of instant yeast, you'll need to activate the yeast by adding it directly to the cooled milk mixture and letting it sit for about 10 minutes before you add the dry dough ingredients mixture.) Stir the dough until everything is thoroughly combined. Cover the bowl with plastic wrap or a clean towel. If it's cold outside, you should make the dough the evening before you want to

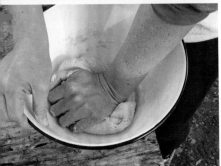

eat the sticky buns. Then place the dough in your cooler or a safe spot and continue in the morning. If it's warm outside, or you can find a warm spot (like inside a car), then set the dough aside to rise for about an hour, or until it's doubled in size.

While the dough is rising, line the inside of the Dutch oven with aluminum foil.

Next, make the glaze. In a small pot (you can just use the same one you heated the milk in) over low heat, combine the butter and maple syrup. Warm the mixture until the butter melts. Pour mixture into the bottom of the Dutch oven. Sprinkle the pecans, brown sugar, and salt on top of the mixture, and set aside.

Lightly flour a clean surface and transfer the dough to it. Pat the dough into a large rectangle, about 16 inches by 12 inches (it doesn't have to be perfect!). This is a very soft dough, so be gentle and handle it with confidence. Sprinkle the filling mixture all across the dough, leaving about an inch on the edge of one long side of the rectangle uncovered. Starting at long side that's sugared, tightly roll up the dough, pinching the last inch of the dough to seal the seam. Place the log of dough seam side down and, using a sharp knife, cut log into 2-inch sections. You should end up with 8 to 10 rounds.

Evenly space out the rounds on top of the glaze in the Dutch oven, keeping a little space between them. Place the lid on the Dutch oven, and let the dough rise for about 30 minutes while you get your campfire going.

Once the buns have started to rise and touch each other, it's time to bake them. How long the rising takes is highly dependent on the weather—so keep an eye on them. The warmer it is, the faster the process will happen. Set the Dutch oven on a grate over a campfire (or shove your fire to the side and place it on the bottom of your fire pit). Place about 14 coals on top of the Dutch oven and none on the bottom. (Using coals on top only should create enough heat to bake the buns, and help avoid burning the sticky sugar topping on the bottom of the Dutch oven.)

Bake for 15 to 25 minutes, carefully rotating the lid a quarter turn once or twice during the baking time. (The cooking time varies depending on the size and quantity of your coals, so check the buns after about 5 minutes to determine how quickly they are

cooking. Adjust the number of coals as necessary to either increase or decrease the heat.) When the buns are just starting to brown on the top and a knife inserted in the center of a bun comes out clean, they're done.

Carefully remove the sticky buns from the Dutch oven by lifting the aluminum foil. Place a plate on the current *top* side, and flip upside down so the plate is now on the bottom. Peel the aluminum foil off to reveal the beautiful glaze that will now be on top.

Serve hot, with a cup of coffee, tea, or hot chocolate.

Dutch Oven Quiche Casserole

Yield: 6 to 8 servings

Prep Time: 20 minutes

Cook Time: 30 to 45 minutes

8 eggs

1½ cups water for hash browns

1 (4.2-ounce) carton dehydrated hash browns

2 tablespoons extra-virgin olive oil

1 cup grated Gruyère cheese

1 cup milk

²/₃ cup mayonnaise

2 cups broccoli, chopped small

²/₃ cup chopped cooked bacon (about 8 strips)

½ teaspoon kosher salt

½ teaspoon freshly ground black pepper

FOR THE BISCUITS

2 cups all-purpose flour

3 teaspoons baking powder

½ teaspoon kosher salt

½ teaspoon freshly ground black pepper

¼ cup butter or margarine, softened

¾ cup buttermilk

½ cup grated Gruyère cheese

TOOLS

Car Camping Base Kit

12-inch Dutch oven

Large mixing bowl

Lid lifter

Saucepan

Heatproof gloves

Our family makes quiche on special occasions, and it's a tradition on Christmas morning. This recipe is a variation of our family quiche recipe—one of the only recipes that I have on an index card, handwritten by my mom. You can make a standard quiche in a Dutch oven, but if we're going to start a campfire and enjoy a slow morning, we like to go big. This is a hybrid of quiche and your typical hungry man Dutch oven breakfast: hash browns as the crust, quiche filling in the center, and buttermilk biscuits thrown on top. I used broccoli, bacon, and Gruyère here, but you can choose what you like. Sausage, Swiss chard, and cheddar is another combination we love. —*Emily*

Buttermilk is an ingredient worth transporting for biscuits like these, but you can make your own buttermilk by mixing ¾ cup milk with 1 tablespoon of lemon juice or vinegar, and letting it sit for about 10 minutes. This even works with vegan alternative like soy milk.

AT HOME

Prepare the dry ingredients for the biscuits. In a ziplock bag, measure out the flour, baking powder, salt, and pepper.

Crack eggs into a Mason jar and keep chilled until ready to use.

AT CAMP

In a small saucepan, bring 1½ cups of water to a boil over high heat, then pour it into the dehydrated hash brown box. Close and set aside for a minimum of 12 minutes.

Add the oil to the Dutch oven, coating the bottom. Add the hash browns, spreading them evenly across the bottom of the Dutch oven. This will act as your crust.

Scramble the eggs by shaking the jar. In a large bowl, combine the eggs, cheese, milk, and mayonnaise. Fold in the broccoli, bacon, salt, and pepper. Pour this egg mixture over the top of the hash browns.

In the ziplock bag containing the biscuit dry ingredients, add the butter and massage the bag until the mixure is crumbly. Add the buttermilk and cheese, and massage until the whole thing is just combined.

Scoop spoonfuls of dough and drop across the top of the egg mixture until it is covered.

Prepare your oven to reach 375°F by placing approximately 18 coals on top and 9 coals underneath. Bake for 30 to 45 minutes, or until the biscuits are brown and eggs are cooked through.

APPETIZERS

Campfire Baked Brie

Yield: 6 to 8 servings
Prep Time: 5 minutes
Cook Time: 15 minutes

1 (8-ounce) wheel of Brie
¼ cup chopped pecans
1 tablespoon brown sugar

FOR SERVING

Buttery crackers

TOOLS

Car Camping Base Kit
8- or 10-inch cast iron skillet
Heatproof gloves

There are a few foods that always create a veritable feeding frenzy. One is freshly made guacamole, and another is baked Brie. It's good to be the cook in these cases, because otherwise, it is very likely you'll get left behind without so much as a bite if you don't know about its appearance right away. It took a little tweaking to come up with a process that works well over the campfire, but this one is a beauty. The pecans toast up in the skillet as the cheese finishes warming through, and the brown sugar at the end melts right in just as you slice the cheese open to cue the frenzy. You'll serve this right out of the skillet and the cast iron will keep the cheese warm for a long time—not that it will last long! —*Emily*

Place the wheel of cheese in a cast iron skillet. Set the skillet on the grate of your campfire and heat over medium heat. The bottom of the cheese wheel will begin to soften faster than the top. When it starts to sizzle out into the skillet, after about 5 minutes, flip the wheel. Add pecans alongside the cheese and let them toast, being careful not to burn them. After about 3 minutes, the whole wheel should have softened and the pecans will have toasted. Remove the skillet from the heat.

Leaving the Brie in the skillet to keep it warm, cut an × in the center, and sprinkle the brown sugar inside. With a small spoon, scoop up the pecans and add into the slit. Serve right out of the skillet alongside some buttery crackers, reminding people to be careful not to burn themselves.

Hot Kale Artichoke Dip

Yield: 8 servings

Prep Time: 10 minutes

Cook Time: 20 minutes

8 ounces cream cheese, softened

8 ounces plain Greek yogurt

$2/3$ cup shredded Parmesan

$1/2$ cup of milk or water

5 cloves garlic, minced

$1/2$ teaspoon kosher salt

$1/2$ teaspoon freshly ground black pepper

1 (14-ounce) can quartered artichokes, drained and roughly chopped

1 (14-ounce) can of white beans, drained

1 bunch kale, stemmed and chopped

Kosher salt and freshly ground black pepper, to taste

FOR SERVING

Tortilla chips or crostini

TOOLS

Car Camping Base Kit

10-inch cast iron skillet

Heatproof gloves

We teach outdoor cooking workshops throughout the year, and we like to offer appetizers that can be made quickly to get our participants warmed up to the process. We made this appetizer at a Campfire Cooking workshop near Mount Baldy, California. Everyone showed up around sunset as the chill settled into the air, and Hot Kale Artichoke Dip proved the perfect transition. We'd lit up the campsite with lanterns and LED tea light candles—our signature move—making it a satisfying night for all the senses. —Mai-Yan

In a large bowl, combine the cream cheese, yogurt, Parmesan, milk, garlic, salt, and pepper. Mix until the ingredients are thoroughly combined.

Place a cast iron skillet on a grate over a medium fire. Add the artichokes, beans, and kale. Pour the cream cheese mixture on top and mix well. Heat the dip, stirring often, until it's hot and bubbly, about 15 minutes. Remove from heat and season to taste with additional salt and pepper. Serve immediately with tortilla chips or crostini.

Roasted Salsa Bean Dip

Yield: 8 servings

Prep Time: 5 minutes

Cook Time: 25 minutes

3 medium tomatoes, whole

½ onion, roughly chopped

3 to 4 cloves garlic, peeled

1 jalapeño, whole, stem chopped off

1 small lemon or lime, halved

½ teaspoon kosher salt

½ teaspoon freshly ground black pepper

1 (28-ounce) can refried beans

½ cup cheddar cheese, shredded (optional)

FOR SERVING

Tortilla chips

TOOLS

Car Camping Base Kit (be sure you included the can opener!)

10-inch cast iron skillet

Heatproof gloves

Most of my trips include a day full of activities, so I get back to camp cold and starving. It's stressful to jump right into starting the fire and rushing dinner onto the table (or laps), while adding on layers of clothing and finding a darn headlamp before it gets too dark. Roasted Salsa Bean Dip is an appetizer that can be cooked on the grate at the same time as building up a campfire, and it's easy enough to hand off to just about anyone so you can focus on dinner. Also, it can be eaten straight from the skillet as soon as it's done, so people are satisfied and occupied more quickly.

Jalapeños become milder when roasted, and the heat is also tempered by the refried beans. However, if you are concerned about spice levels, choose a milder chile, such as an Anaheim or poblano. If you're looking for more intensity, throw in an extra jalapeño or choose a serrano. You can always taste a bit of the chile before adding it to the skillet to get an idea of the spice level. —*Emily*

Put the tomatoes, onion, garlic, and jalapeño into a cast iron skillet and heat over medium-high heat. (If you're using a campfire, you want flames directly under the grate.) Let the ingredients char and pop and soften, stirring occasionally, for about 15 minutes. Using a fork, juice the lemon into the mixture. Discard the peel. Mash the mixture with a fork until it looks like a nice, chunky salsa. (No need to remove skins or seeds on anything.) Add salt and pepper, and taste for balance. Add the beans, stirring to combine, and continue to heat until the mixture has melted together and starts to bubble, about 10 minutes. Top with shredded cheese, if desired, and serve with tortilla chips.

HOT KALE ARTICHOKE DIP (PG 94)

ROASTED SALSA BEAN DIP (PG 95)

EMBER-ROASTED BABA GHANOUSH (PG 98)

Ember-Roasted Baba Ghanoush

Yield: About 2 cups

Prep Time: 15 minutes

Cook Time: 10 minutes

1 large eggplant

1 clove of garlic

½ teaspoon kosher salt, plus more to taste

2 to 4 tablespoons tahini

Juice of 1 medium lemon

FOR SERVING

Extra-virgin olive oil

Chopped fresh Italian parsley

Pita bread

TOOLS

Car Camping Base Kit

Heatproof gloves

Towel

Medium mixing bowl

Potato masher or fork

You don't have to make every piece of a meal from scratch as long as you have one or two impressive from-scratch elements. This simple and elegant baba ghanoush sets the tone for that scenario, rounding out a meze platter of supermarket hummus, dolmas, tabbouleh, and pita bread. You'll get to utilize the campfire in an impressive way, but will quickly get down to enjoying an evening of entertaining under the stars. —*Emily*

Wrap the eggplant tightly in aluminum foil, and place it directly on the embers of a campfire. Roast the eggplant until it's softened, turning often with tongs, about 10 minutes. Set aside to cool.

While the eggplant is cooling, finely mince the garlic and then sprinkle the salt over the top of it. Gather the mixture into a pile and, holding your knife at a 30-degree angle to the board, scrape your knife across the board, smashing the garlic. Repeat this process until the garlic is broken down into a paste. Set aside.

Once the eggplant is cool enough to handle, place it on a cutting board and slice off the top stem. Cut the eggplant lengthwise in quarters. Scrape off the skin and discard, and place the flesh in a towel. Drain off any liquid that is released and then return the eggplant to the cutting board. Chop the eggplant as finely as possible and place it in the bowl.

Add the salted garlic paste to the bowl of eggplant, along with 2 tablespoons of tahini and 2 tablespoons of the lemon juice. Mix well to combine. Taste and add additional tahini, lemon juice, and salt if needed. Drizzle with olive oil, sprinkle with chopped parsley, and serve with hot pita bread.

Spiced Nuts with Shallots

Yield: About 5 cups
Prep Time: 5 minutes
Cook Time: 15 to 20 minutes

2 tablespoons extra-virgin olive oil

1 pound raw mixed nuts

2 shallots, peeled and thinly sliced

6 cloves garlic, peeled and thinly sliced

2 teaspoons paprika

1 tablespoon maple syrup

Sea salt, to taste

TOOLS

Car Camping Base Kit

10- or 12-inch cast iron skillet

Heatproof gloves

These warm, toasted nuts are salty and sweet, with bits of crispy shallots and garlic mixed in. They were so delicious with a cold beer after a day of superbloom viewing in Anza-Borrego that if there hadn't been such a big crowd of people to share with, we probably would have just eaten nuts for dinner. Make it earlier in the day so the nuts are warming on the campfire as people come back to camp for the evening. —*Aimee*

Heat the oil in a cast iron skillet on a grate set over a campfire. Add the nuts, shallots, garlic, and paprika. Stir well to combine and continue cooking, stirring frequently, until the shallots and garlic are crispy and the nuts are toasted, about 15 to 20 minutes. Drizzle the nuts with the syrup and sprinkle with a healthy shake of salt. Taste and adjust seasonings. When you're done cooking the nuts, remove from the fire to serve straight out of the skillet. (If you'd like to serve directly over the campfire, move the logs to the other side so you can enjoy the warmth without burning the nuts.)

Goat Cheese Stuffed Mini Sweet Peppers

Yield: 4 servings

Prep Time: 10 minutes

Cook Time: 5 to 10 minutes

16 mini bell peppers

5 ounces goat cheese

1 tablespoon fresh herbs (such as chives, basil, sage, or thyme), finely chopped

Kosher salt and freshly ground black pepper

3 tablespoons extra-virgin olive oil

TOOLS

Car Camping Base Kit

Heatproof gloves

This is a variation on the very first recipe we ever posted on Dirty Gourmet back in 2009, and it still holds up. The idea came about on a recipe testing camping trip in San Clemente where we ended up making fourteen dishes. The only problem was that there were only the three of us to eat all the food! Feel free to experiment with the filling. You could try using cream cheese, ricotta, or a mixture of whatever cheese you find in your fridge, and then go crazy with herbs and spices. —*Mai-Yan*

Place the peppers on a 12-inch length of aluminum foil. Cut a slit lengthwise down each pepper. (The slit should only cut through one side of the pepper, not all the way through, so that you can access the hollow area inside.) Set aside.

In a small bowl, combine the cheese and herbs with a pinch of salt and pepper, and mix well. Transfer the cheese-herb mixture to a ziplock bag and seal. Cut off a corner of the bag to turn it into a piping bag.

Pry open a pepper with your fingers and stick the piping bag into the slit. Pipe the cheese mixture into the pepper. Repeat with all the peppers.

Center the stuffed peppers on the aluminum foil and drizzle with the oil. Fold over the foil to create a closed pouch, making sure to seal the seams tightly (see the Appendix for instructions.)

Place the foil packet on a grate over the fire or directly on the embers. Watch closely, making sure to rotate the packet often. Roast the peppers until they're beginning to char on one or two sides and the cheese is hot, about 5 to 10 minutes.

Warm Olives with Fennel and Orange

Yield: 6 to 8 servings
Prep Time: 5 minutes
Cook Time: 10 to 15 minutes

2 cups green olives, preferably unpitted

¼ cup extra-virgin olive oil

1 head fennel, chopped

Zest of 1 orange

2 teaspoons fennel seeds

TOOLS

Car Camping Base Kit
Vegetable peeler
10- or 12-inch cast iron skillet
Heatproof gloves

We love to throw car camping parties. It doesn't take much to make things feel fancy when you're outdoors, and the efforts go a long way. These olives are inspired by a recipe in *Camp Sunset* but are served warmed on a grate over a campfire. The fennel browns at the edges and gets just a little chewy, while the orange-infused olives get smoked by the fire. Pair them with our Spiced Nuts with Shallots (see Car Camping, Appetizers) and you have yourself a party! —*Aimee*

Combine the olives, oil, chopped fennel, orange zest, and fennel seeds in a cast iron skillet. Set the skillet on a grate set over a campfire and cook until the mixture is heated through and the fennel is lightly browned, about 10 to 15 minutes.

Foil Packet Nachos

Yield: 4 servings

Prep Time: 5 to 10 minutes

Cook Time: 10 minutes

1 (12-ounce) bag of tortilla chips

1 (8-ounce) bag of Mexican blend shredded cheese

1 (8-ounce) can of black beans

OPTIONAL GARNISHES

1 (16-ounce) jar of chunky salsa

8 ounces sour cream

4 scallions, chopped

1 jalapeño, sliced

Cilantro

Cotija cheese

Grilled chicken

TOOLS

Car Camping Base Kit

The Panamint mountain range is just outside of Death Valley National Park. At the base of these mountains is a ghost town called Ballarat. This is where I first met Aimee and Kismat on their family's annual New Year's camping trip. The wind showed up to the party suddenly and ripped Aimee's new tent in half. Using her embroidering supplies, we spent the next hour getting to know each other while sewing the tent body back onto its base. This trip not only formed a friendship but inspired the first version of camping nachos. Since then, all three of us have experimented with different versions, trying ground beef, black beans, pinto beans, store-bought salsa, homemade pico de gallo, and the list goes on. The final verdict—it's *all* good. In that spirit, this Foil Packet Nachos recipe is very loose and is mostly about execution. The foil packet creates a mini oven so you can get your chips super crunchy and your cheese extra melty. We encourage you to garnish with any and all of your favorite toppings. —*Mai-Yan*

Cut 4 sheets of aluminum foil about 12 inches long. Lay flat and stack. (Each piece will become an individual serving foil packet.)

Place about 15 to 20 tortilla chips in the center of one sheet of aluminum foil. Sprinkle chips with ¼ to ½ cup of cheese. Add 3 tablespoons of black beans, and tightly fold the foil into an aluminum foil pouch (see the Appendix for directions). Repeat for remaining aluminum foil sheets.

Place prepared foil packets directly into fire pit next to a medium-hot fire, but not in direct flames, for about 5 minutes. Then turn the foil packets 180 degrees so the opposite side of each foil packet is closest to fire. Nachos are ready when cheese has melted, about another 5 minutes. Remove from heat.

Carefully open up foil packets and use them like a bowl. Garnish nachos with salsa, sour cream, scallions, jalapeños, or whatever suits your taste buds.

FOIL PACKET NACHOS (PG 103)

BROWN SUGAR BALSAMIC ROASTED GARLIC

Brown Sugar Balsamic Roasted Garlic

Yield: About ½ cup
Prep Time: 5 minutes
Cook Time: 30 to 40 minutes

5 heads garlic
1 tablespoon extra-virgin olive oil
2 teaspoons brown sugar
2 teaspoons balsamic vinegar
½ teaspoon kosher salt

FOR SERVING

Toasted bread or crackers
Goat cheese

TOOLS

Car Camping Base Kit
Small mixing bowl

The first time I made roasted garlic in a campfire, I threw aluminum foil–wrapped pouches of garlic directly in the hottest part of the fire. After about half an hour, I opened up my pouches and was sure it was unusable. It all burned! I forced myself to push on and see if I could turn my flop into something edible, and once I got past the charred outer layers of papery skin, I found perfectly roasted garlic. Now, roasted garlic is delicious on its own, but mixing it with some sweet brown sugar and tart balsamic vinegar, turns it into an impressive appetizer. You'll probably end up with some black flecks of burned garlic skin in the final dish, but that's OK. Those bits add a smoky depth of flavor that you can't get in your oven at home. —*Aimee*

Peel off any loose, papery skins of the garlic, leaving the head whole. Slice off about a ½ inch of the top of the garlic, exposing most of the cloves.

Place the garlic heads on a 12-inch length of aluminum foil, drizzling the exposed cloves with the oil. Wrap the garlic tightly in the foil.

Place the foil-wrapped garlic directly in the embers of a campfire. Roast the garlic, turning often with long tongs. After about 10 minutes, peek into the foil pouch to check to make sure the garlic is not burning. Adjust the position of the garlic as needed to keep it from burning. Roast until the garlic is very soft and slightly browned, about 20 to 30 more minutes.

Set the garlic aside until it's cool enough to handle. Remove from the foil, then squeeze the garlic cloves out of their papers directly into a bowl. With a fork, mash the garlic, then stir in the brown sugar, vinegar, and salt. Taste and adjust the seasoning.

Serve with hot toasted bread or crackers and goat cheese.

Variation: Lemon Parsley Roasted Garlic

Omit the brown sugar and balsamic vinegar. Instead stir in 1 tablespoon minced Italian parsley and the zest and juice of about half a small lemon.

Tomato and Jalapeño Toasts

Yield: 8 to 10 toasts

Prep Time: 10 minutes at home, 5 minutes at camp

Cook Time: 5 to 10 minutes

1 baguette, halved lengthwise and cut into 4- to 6-inch pieces

1 clove garlic, halved

4 tablespoons extra-virgin olive oil

2 large ripe tomatoes, sliced

FOR THE PASTE

2 small lemons

1 small lime

3 jalapeños, stemmed and seeded

2 teaspoons kosher salt

TOOLS

Car Camping Base Kit

On a trip to the Mojave Preserve with Mai-Yan, I brought along the ingredients to make Spanish Pan Con Tomate, which is, traditionally, bread rubbed with tomato and seasoned with salt and olive oil. I thought it would be a fun and simple appetizer to make over a campfire, so we started to make it when Mai-Yan remembered she had some Jalapeño Citrus Paste she was recipe testing. We couldn't leave well enough alone and tried topping our tomato toasts with it. We never went back to eating the plain tomato version again! Just note that the Jalapeño Citrus Paste is spicy and salty, so a little goes a long way. —*Aimee*

AT HOME

Prepare the jalapeño paste: With a vegetable peeler, peel sections of lemon and lime peel. In the bowl of a food processor fitted with the metal blade attachment, place the peel, jalapeños, and salt. Process until a paste is formed. Keep chilled until ready to use.

AT CAMP

On a grate set over a campfire over medium-high heat, toast the baguette pieces. Remove from the fire and rub the cut side of each toast with the cut side of a clove of garlic. Drizzle with oil, then spread a very thin layer of the jalapeño paste. Top with sliced tomatoes.

Eat immediately, or return the toasts to the campfire to warm up the toppings just a bit.

SIDE DISHES

Grilled Green Bean Salad

Yield: 4 servings
Prep Time: 15 minutes
Cook Time: 10 minutes

1 tablespoon extra-virgin olive oil

1 pound French green beans

1 red bell pepper, julienned

1 tablespoon chopped garlic

FOR THE DRESSING

2 tablespoons extra-virgin olive oil

Zest and juice of 1 medium lemon

½ teaspoon Dijon mustard

½ teaspoon kosher salt

½ teaspoon freshly ground black pepper

TOOLS

Car Camping Base Kit

10-inch cast iron skillet

Large mixing bowl

Heatproof gloves

We made this recipe for an event where we cooked for two-hundred people for four days. We rarely get to use "the grizzly"—our sixteen-inch Dutch oven weighing in at thirty-six pounds empty—but we filled it up at least five times for this recipe. We even had a couple other Dutch ovens going at the same time. It's unexpected to have a salad that combines grilled vegetables with crunchy fresh ones. But these kinds of salads hold up well and can even be eaten as a trail dish the next day. —*Emily*

AT HOME

Make the dressing: In a jar, add the oil, lemon zest and juice, mustard, salt, and pepper. Close the lid and pack in your cooler.

AT CAMP

Add the oil to a cast iron skillet over high heat. Add the green beans and cook, tossing occasionally, until bright green and tender, but also starting to blister and char a bit, about 10 minutes. Take your jar of dressing out of the cooler and shake to emulsify. Add bell peppers, garlic, and dressing to the beans and toss.

Remove from heat, and transfer into a large bowl for serving.

Salt and Vinegar Roasted Potatoes

Yield: 4 servings

Prep Time: 5 minutes

Cook Time: 20 to 30 minutes

1½ pounds yellow potatoes, quartered

4 tablespoons extra-virgin olive oil

3 tablespoons white vinegar

1 tablespoon fresh thyme, chopped

1 teaspoon kosher salt

TOOLS

Car Camping Base Kit

12-inch cast iron skillet with 12-inch Dutch oven lid

Lid lifter

Heatproof gloves

Wes and I got married at a farmhouse in the mountains outside of Santa Barbara. The venue was perfect for us because it came with no required catering package, there was enough space to sleep our whole wedding party, and the location was so beautiful that it needed basically nothing for décor. Instead, we spent our weekend focusing on celebrating with our friends. Of course, Dirty Gourmet catered the whole four-day event. For the main wedding dinner, we made gin-marinated roasted fingerlings that we were told changed some people's lives. This recipe is a variation of that one. Simple is good while camping, and this is as simple as it gets for a campfire recipe. —*Emily*

Place potatoes in one layer in a cast iron skillet. Add the oil and vinegar. Sprinkle the thyme and salt across the potatoes, and then stir to coat evenly.

Set the skillet on the grate of a campfire with a hot fire underneath. Place the lid on top and add 14 coals on top. Cook, stirring occasionally, until potatoes are crispy and golden on the outside, and soft on the inside, about 20 to 30 minutes.

Grilled Spiced Cauliflower Steaks

Yield: 5 servings

Prep Time: 10 minutes

Cook Time: 10 to 15 minutes

7 cloves garlic, minced

4 tablespoons extra-virgin olive oil

1 teaspoon kosher salt

½ teaspoon smoked paprika

½ teaspoon freshly ground black pepper

½ teaspoon chili powder

½ teaspoon oregano

1 head of cauliflower, leaves trimmed

TOOLS

Car Camping Base Kit

I tend to overcomplicate things, especially when I'm in recipe testing mode. I work to come up with a dish that no one (not even the internet!) has ever heard of and that has complex layers of flavors and textures. But I'm always amazed at how delicious simple vegetables can be, and each time I rediscover this I vow to spend more time enjoying them. This recipe is lovely *and* restrained. Cauliflower is a hearty blank slate for flavor, and the campfire's smoky addition pairs well with the combination of spices chosen for the dish. Eat it alongside our Steak and Veggie Skewers with Harissa (see Car Camping, Entrees), or as a light main with pita and hummus. —*Emily*

In a small bowl, combine garlic, oil, salt, paprika, black pepper, chili powder, and oregano. Mix well.

Place cauliflower on a cutting board with stem base flat. Working parallel to the stem, cut into 1-inch slabs. (You should end up with about 4 slabs and then a handful of loose florets.)

Cut one piece of aluminum foil at least double the size of each cauliflower slab and one for the loose florets. Place each cauliflower slab on top of a piece of aluminum foil and generously slather all sides with the spice paste. Neatly wrap each cauliflower slab so the aluminum foil is tight but so it is possible to unwrap it during the cooking process. Use any remaining spice paste for the loose florets and prepare the same way. Neatly fold down the top of each foil pouch and then the remaining two openings on the sides.

Place the cauliflower directly onto the embers of a waning campfire. (You can push the coals over to one side if you're still enjoying the flames.) Cook the cauliflower for about 5 minutes, and then flip the foil pouches. You should hear a nice sizzle! Cook for another 5 minutes. Open up the foil pouches to check on the cauliflower. You're looking for tender cauliflower with a nicely browned surface and a little charring. Wrap it back up and throw it back on the fire, for another 5 minutes if the cauliflower is not quite there yet. Serve piping hot.

GRILLED SPICED CAULIFLOWER STEAKS (PG 111)

BAKED BEANS

Baked Beans

Yield: About 8 servings
Prep Time: 10 minutes
Cook Time: 4 to 5 hours

1 pound dried navy beans, soaked overnight

1 medium onion, minced

½ cup maple syrup

¼ cup molasses

¼ cup apple cider vinegar

2 tablespoons tomato paste

1 tablespoon dried ground ginger

1 tablespoon whole grain mustard

1 teaspoon kosher salt

½ teaspoon freshly ground black pepper

TOOLS

Car Camping Base Kit

10-inch Dutch oven

Heatproof gloves

Lid lifter

Baked beans take a while to do completely at camp, but it can be done if you've got the time. A good method is to start the day before and finish the day you'll be eating them. This recipe is written as for campfire-only preparation mainly because you could run out of fuel if you make it on a stovetop! Don't forget to soak your beans overnight to help with the process, and be sure your beans are fully cooked before you add the other ingredients to the pot. Otherwise, they may not get completely tender even after hours of baking. —Aimee

Drain the soaked beans and place them in a 10-inch Dutch oven, adding enough fresh water to cover them a couple of inches. Cover the Dutch oven.

Set the Dutch oven on a grate over a high-heat campfire, bringing the water to a boil. Once boiling, adjust the position of the coals under the grate so that the mixture can reduce to a simmer. Simmer until the beans are completely cooked, about 1 to 2 hours, checking on them occasionally to make sure the water hasn't evaporated, adding more water as needed.

Once the beans are softened, check the water level again. Drain off any excess of one inch of cooking water, reserving the spare water in a separate container. Add the onion, maple syrup, molasses, vinegar, tomato paste, ginger, mustard, salt, and pepper. Stir to combine, cover, and then place the mixture back on the grate or directly in the fire pit, pushing the coals to the side so the mixture won't burn on the bottom or sides of the Dutch oven. Place about 15 coals on the top of the Dutch oven.

Cook for about 3 hours, stirring regularly to make sure the beans don't burn. If the beans start to dry out on the top, stir in some of the reserved cooking water. When the sauce forms a sticky glaze, taste and adjust the seasoning with additional salt, pepper, and apple cider vinegar.

Campfire Grilled Corn with Ancho Lime Mayo and Cilantro

Yield: 6 ears

Prep Time: 10 minutes

Cook Time: 15 to 20 minutes

6 ears corn, shucked

2 tablespoons butter, cut into 6 pats

Kosher salt, to taste

Freshly ground black pepper, to taste

FOR THE SPICY MAYO

1/2 cup mayonnaise

Juice from half a lime

1 teaspoon ancho chile powder, or similar

1/3 cup cilantro leaves, chopped

TOOLS

Car Camping Base Kit

Small mixing bowl

Corn season is one of the most exciting times of the year for me. It hurts a bit to pay a dollar for two ears of corn when I know that eventually I'll get twelve for the same price. I remember going to the farmers' market with my grandmother in North Carolina and watching the farmers standing on a mountain of corn, tossing the good ones down to us.

Grilled corn is the best kind, but that still doesn't answer all the debates about how best to cook it: directly on the grate with no husk, soaked and then cooked on the grill in its husk, or pre-buttered, salted, and peppered and wrapped in foil. Though the first two options create a more photogenic grilled corn, the foil option makes the best tasting corn. My uncle Steve taught me that one, and he is right. He knows his grillin'. If you've never tried mayo on your corn, you may think it sounds strange (I did), but trust me. —*Emily*

AT HOME

Make the spicy mayonnaise: In a small bowl, place the mayonnaise, lime juice, and ancho chile powder, and mix. Spoon into an airtight container and keep chilled until ready to use.

AT CAMP

Cut six pieces of aluminum foil that will fit around an ear of corn. Place each ear of corn in a piece of foil, adding a pat of butter and a sprinkle of salt and pepper to each.

On the grate of a campfire at medium-high heat, grill the corn for about 15 minutes, rotating several times.

Unwrap an ear and check for doneness. Corn is done when it has a little give to it. You may have to taste test one to be sure. It's OK if you get a few little charred spots on the corn. This is the best part.

Slather the corn with spicy mayo and sprinkle with cilantro. Add an extra sprinkle of chile powder, if desired.

Skillet Cornbread with Bacon and Chiles

Yield: 8 servings

Prep Time: 5 minutes

Cook Time: 40 to 50 minutes

1 cup cornmeal

1 cup all-purpose flour

⅓ cup sugar

2 teaspoons baking powder

1 teaspoon kosher salt

3 Anaheim chiles

5 strips bacon

6 tablespoons butter

1¼ cups milk

TOOLS

Car Camping Base Kit

Container with a lid or foil

10-inch cast iron skillet

Lid for your skillet or aluminum foil

Heatproof gloves

Joshua Tree for Thanksgiving weekend is a holiday tradition among climbers. We don't get to participate every year ourselves but are always excited when the chance arises. One year, I cooked up a miniature Thanksgiving meal for just a few friends. We brought giant turkey legs to cook on the grate and made this cornbread as well. Roasted Anaheim chiles are a delicious addition to any recipe. And then there's bacon. Use pre-cooked bacon if you want to eliminate a step. —*Mai-Yan*

AT HOME

In a ziplock bag, combine the cornmeal, flour, sugar, baking powder, and salt.

AT CAMP

Roast the chiles on the grate directly over the flames of your campfire or stovetop. Rotate the chiles until the skin is blistered and charred on all sides. Set aside to cool.

When they're cool enough to handle, peel the skin off the chiles and remove the stem and seeds, discarding all. Roughly chop the chiles, and set aside.

In a cast iron skillet over medium-high heat, cook the bacon until crispy. Remove from heat and transfer bacon onto paper towels to cool slightly. Break up in small bits, and set aside. Drain most of the fat from the skillet. Add the butter. When it's melted, pour all but about a tablespoon of it into a large mixing bowl. The remaining butter will grease the skillet.

Add the milk and cornmeal mixture in the large mixing bowl, and stir to combine. Be careful not to overmix the batter, or your cornbread might get tough. Stir in the roasted chiles and crumbled bacon.

Place the skillet over medium heat. When heated, pour in the batter. Reduce the heat to low and cover the skillet with a tight-fitting lid or foil. Cook over low heat for 25 to 35 minutes. The cornbread is done when a knife or toothpick inserted into the center comes out clean.

Remove the skillet from the heat and serve immediately. If you aren't going to serve the cornbread right away, run a knife around the outside of the skillet and invert the cornbread onto a cutting board. This way it won't continue to cook in the hot skillet.

Dutch Oven Jeweled Rice

Yield: 8 servings

Prep Time: 5 minutes

Cook Time: 30 minutes

2 tablespoons butter

1 large onion, chopped

1 teaspoon turmeric

1 teaspoon ground cardamom

1⅓ cups basmati rice

2⅔ cups chicken or vegetable broth

½ cup pistachios, chopped

½ cup currants

4 green onions, chopped

TOOLS

Car Camping Base Kit

10-inch Dutch oven

Lid lifter

Heatproof gloves

For a catered campout we hosted at Kirby Cove in San Francisco, we cooked the rice in Dutch ovens in a giant fire pit, right in front of our seventy-five hungry guests. It was invigorating to teach as we cooked, and this Jeweled Rice was a delicious part of the evening's Mediterranean meal. Afterward, we realized that we never actually tested the recipe before we cooked it! We laughed about how daring a move this was for us, but it just goes to show how forgiving Dutch oven cooking is. Since that fateful event, we've cooked Dutch oven rice for large groups many times, and each time I'm amazed at how magical it seems: even with an oven piled high with hot coals, the water still barely simmers, but after the right amount of time, the lid opens to a pot of perfectly cooked rice. —*Emily*

Melt the butter in a 10-inch Dutch oven set on a grate over a campfire over medium heat. Stir in the onion and cook until slightly caramelized and translucent, about 10 minutes. Add the turmeric, cardamom, and rice, stirring to coat the rice in the butter. Stir in the broth. Cover and bring to a simmer, adjusting the coals as necessary. Continue to simmer for about 20 minutes, until the rice is cooked through. Remove from the heat, and stir in the pistachios and currants. Cover and let sit for about 5 minutes. Sprinkle with green onions and serve.

ENTREES

One Pot Pasta Puttanesca

Yield: 6 servings

Prep Time: 10 minutes

Cook Time: 20 minutes

¹/₄ cup extra-virgin olive oil

6 cloves garlic, minced

¹/₂ teaspoon red chile flakes

4 cups vegetable broth

1 (28-ounce) can crushed tomatoes

1 pound rigatoni

¹/₂ cup good-quality pitted black olives, chopped

2 tablespoons capers

FOR SERVING

Chopped fresh Italian parsley

Freshly grated Parmesan cheese

TOOLS

Car Camping Base Kit

Large pot

My mom once poured a boiling pot of water on her sock-plus-sandal covered foot in an attempt to drain pasta in the Sierra backcountry. She spent the rest of the trip with her foot soaking in the icy cold creek near our campsite. Somehow she managed to hike out a couple days later, but it was a pretty terrible burn to withstand. I've been wary of draining hot water off of anything ever since, so I'm motivated to find ways to avoid it altogether. Case in point: This pasta cooks in its own sauce and requires no draining at all. It'll look soupy for a while, but then suddenly the pasta absorbs all the extra water and a sauce will form. If you have any leftover, break out your pie iron and make a spaghetti sandwich. —*Aimee*

In a large pot, heat the oil over medium heat. Add the garlic and cook, stirring often, until it's slightly browned at the edges, about 2 to 3 minutes. Add the chile flakes and stir for another minute. Add the broth, tomatoes, rigatoni, olives, and capers. Cover the pot and bring to a boil. Reduce the heat to low and simmer, partially covered, stirring occasionally for 8 to 10 minutes or until the pasta is al dente.

Serve with fresh Italian parsley and Parmesan cheese.

Smoky Sausage and White Bean Stew

Yield: 6 servings

Prep Time: 20 minutes

Cook Time: 1 hour

3 tablespoons extra-virgin olive oil, divided

1 pound Italian sausages, sliced into ¼-inch rounds

1 medium onion, chopped

2 celery stalks, chopped

1 fennel bulb, chopped

3 cloves garlic, minced

1 tablespoon chopped fresh thyme

2 teaspoons smoked paprika

1 teaspoon ground cumin

¼ teaspoon cayenne pepper, or more to taste

1 (28-ounce) can diced tomatoes

2 (14-ounce) cans low-sodium cannellini beans

1 cup water

1 bunch kale, stems and center ribs discarded and leaves roughly chopped

FOR THE DUMPLINGS

2 cups all-purpose flour

1 tablespoon baking powder

1 tablespoon chopped fresh thyme

1 teaspoon garlic powder

¾ teaspoon kosher salt

¾ cup milk

½ cup mayonnaise

TOOLS

Car Camping Base Kit

Large pot

Aimee, Mai-Yan, and I used to work variable schedules, so it was like winning the lottery to get a couple of days in a row to go camping together. Since these opportunities would often come up at the last minute, we usually agreed to make something at home that would reheat easily at camp for the first night. This stew is the ticket! It's smoky and warming and can be cooked at camp as easily as at home before you go. It works well in a Dutch oven on your campfire grate, or on your stovetop. Finish off the stew with the addition of freshly crisped sausage and soft dumplings that taste even better the deeper they sink into the pot. *—Emily*

AT HOME

Prepare the dry ingredients for your dumpling dough: In a large ziplock bag, combine the flour, baking powder, thyme, garlic powder, and salt.

AT CAMP

Heat 2 tablespoons of the oil in a large pot on a grate of a campfire. Add the sausage and sauté until it's cooked through and crispy. Remove sausages from the pot and set aside.

Add the remaining tablespoon of oil to the pot, then add the onion, celery, and fennel. Season with salt and pepper, and cook until softened, stirring occasionally, about 5 minutes. Stir in the garlic, thyme, paprika, cumin, and cayenne, and cook for 1 minute. Add the tomatoes, beans in their juice, and water, and bring to a boil. Cover and simmer for 10 to 15 minutes, stirring occasionally until the vegetables are tender. Add the sausage and kale, cover and simmer, stirring occasionally, while finishing the dumpling dough .

For the dough, add the milk and mayonnaise to the ziplock bag of the biscuits' dry ingredients. Seal the bag and massage the ingredients to combine until dough is uniform in consistency.

Stir the stew once more, then drop rounded tablespoons of dough atop the stew. Cover and simmer for 10 more minutes or until dumplings are fluffy in the center.

Spinach Lentil Soup

Yield: 8 servings

Prep Time: 20 minutes

Cook Time: 45 minutes

3 tablespoons extra-virgin olive oil

1 large onion, diced

1 large carrot, diced

2 plum tomatoes, diced

2 cloves garlic, minced

2 tablespoons tomato paste

Zest and juice of 1 medium lemon

2 teaspoons paprika

1 teaspoon turmeric

8 cups vegetable broth

1⅓ cups green or brown lentils

4 cups baby spinach

Kosher salt and freshly ground black pepper, to taste

FOR SERVING

Crusty bread

Butter

TOOLS

Car Camping Base Kit

Large pot

Every household has its go-to ingredient or dish, and at my house, it's lentils and soup. In fact, whenever I ask Daniel what he wants for dinner, he always replies: "It's never not soup weather!" It's not his best prose, but he firmly stands by this statement. This particular recipe sounds generic, but there's a wild card—lemon zest! These colorful little scraps of lemon peel elevate this soup from standard fare to mouth party. In fact, I have Aimee on record stating: "This is the best soup I've ever had." So there you have it, the official Aimee endorsement. My work is done. —*Mai-Yan*

It's true you don't need fancy tools to cook, but some are really, really nice to have. One such tool is a microplane: a very fine grater that allows you to zest to your heart's content. If you don't have one, you can use a small sharp knife, making sure to get as little pith (the white stuff under the peel) as possible.

Heat the oil in a large pot over medium-high heat. Add the onion and carrot, and sauté until the onions are softened and beginning to brown, about 5 minutes. Add the tomatoes, garlic, tomato paste, and lemon juice. Stir and cook until the tomatoes are broken down and become saucy, about 5 more minutes. Add the paprika and turmeric, and cook for another minute. Add the broth and lentils, and bring to a boil. Reduce the heat to low, cover, and simmer until the lentils are tender, about 30 minutes. Stir in the spinach and lemon zest, and continue cooking until the spinach is wilted, about 5 minutes. Season with salt and pepper, to taste. Serve this soup alongside fresh crusty bread and butter.

Spicy Miso Ramen

Yield: 4 servings

**Prep Time: 15 minutes at home,
15 minutes at camp**

Cook Time: 40 to 45 minutes

FOR THE MISO SOUP BASE

1/2 onion, chopped

1/2 cup miso

2 tablespoons chili-garlic sauce

1-inch piece of ginger, peeled and
roughly chopped

2 tablespoons rice vinegar

1 tablespoon vegetable oil

1/2 tablespoon sesame oil

1 tablespoon soy sauce

FOR THE RAMEN

1 (14-ounce) block extra-firm tofu

4 tablespoons vegetable oil

4 cups vegetable broth

2 cups milk

6 to 10 dried shiitake mushrooms

8 ounces ramen noodles

FOR SERVING

2 to 4 scallions, sliced

Nori seaweed sheets, ripped up

Chili-garlic sauce

Soy sauce, for drizzling

TOOLS

Car Camping Base Kit

12-inch cast iron or nonstick skillet

Large pot

Slotted spoon

Ladle

In the world of backpacking, ramen is to dinner what oatmeal is to breakfast. Even though the packaged stuff is the perfect backup meal because it is compact and inexpensive, it doesn't offer much to love beyond that. Plus, the three of us are from Los Angeles, so we know what *real* ramen can be! This recipe is nothing like the three-for-a-dollar option that stays in my pack for emergencies only. The noodles float in a creamy umami broth that gets better the longer the dried shiitakes simmer. It's a special thing to have a freshly made ramen dish while car camping. —*Emily*

AT HOME

Make the miso soup base: In the bowl of a food processor fitted with the metal blade attachment, place the onion, miso, chili-garlic sauce, ginger, vinegar, oils, and soy sauce, and blend until well combined. Transfer mixture to a jar to transport to camp. Keep chilled.

Press the tofu: Wrap the tofu in a kitchen towel and place it under a heavy object, like a cast iron skillet or meat press, until most of the liquid is out, about 30 minutes. Cut the tofu into 1-inch cubes and transfer to a container to take with you to camp.

AT CAMP

Heat the oil in a skillet over medium-high heat. When the oil is hot, add the cubed tofu and fry until it's golden brown on all sides, about 10 minutes. Add 2 tablespoons of the miso soup base, and stir until tofu is coated, about 1 to 2 minutes. Remove the skillet from the heat and set aside.

In a large pot, combine the broth, milk, and mushrooms, and bring to a boil. Reduce heat to low and simmer until mushrooms have softened, about 20 minutes.

With a slotted spoon, transfer the mushrooms to a cutting board, slice them, and return them to the broth. Add the ramen noodles. Return the broth to a boil. Continue to cook at high heat, stirring occasionally, until ramen is cooked through, about 3 minutes. Add the rest of the miso soup base to the broth, stirring to combine. Let cook just until broth is heated through, about 2 more minutes.

Serve the ramen by using tongs to pull out some noodles and place into big bowls. Then ladle the broth over the noodles and add a scoop of tofu. Top with chopped scallions, seaweed, chili sauce, and a drizzle of soy sauce.

Red Posole

Yield: 6 to 8 servings
Prep Time: 15 minutes
Cook Time: 40 to 50 minutes

3 New Mexico dried chiles

2 tablespoons extra-virgin olive oil

1 large yellow onion, chopped

1/4 cup California mild chili powder

2 teaspoons ground cumin

1 teaspoon kosher salt

10 cloves of garlic, minced

2 teaspoons oregano

2 zucchini or yellow squash, diced

2 (15-ounce) cans pinto beans, drained

2 (15-ounce) cans hominy, drained

6 cups water

Kosher salt and freshly ground black pepper, to taste

FOR THE FRIED TORTILLA TOPPING

1/4 cup canola oil

10 to 12 taco-sized corn tortillas

FOR SERVING

Lime wedges

Shredded cabbage or lettuce

Chopped cilantro

Diced avocado

TOOLS

Car Camping Base Kit

Large pot with lid

Small skillet

Posole is a brothy Mexican soup, usually made with pork and hominy and topped with cabbage, onion, radishes, avocado, and lime juice. We prefer the vegetarian route for camping, and this one can be made quickly and entirely at camp. If you prefer, you can add pork to this version. Just add it when you add the vegetables and hominy to simmer. For this recipe, the toppings are absolutely necessary—especially the lime. We like to make this when we're camping with large groups so we can enlist some helpers to prep the toppings. If you want to make it a bit simpler, you can eliminate the fried tortilla topping prep by bringing packaged tortilla chips. —*Aimee*

Break off the stems of the chiles and shake out as many seeds as you can.

Place the dried chiles in a large pot over high heat, and toast until they darken in color and smell toasted, about 5 minutes. Remove from pot and set aside. Add the oil to the pot, and reduce heat to medium high. Add onion, chili powder, cumin, and salt, and mix well. Cook for about 5 minutes and then add the garlic, oregano, and toasted chiles. Continue to cook mixture until onions are translucent, stirring occasionally, about 7 minutes. Add the zucchini, beans, hominy, and water to the pot, and bring to boil. Reduce heat to low and simmer for about 20 to 30 minutes.

Meanwhile, prepare the fried tortilla topping. Add the oil to a small skillet and heat over medium heat. Fry corn tortillas in the oil, about 2 minutes per side. Remove from skillet, and sprinkle with salt.

Season the posole to taste with salt and pepper. Serve with plenty of lime juice, shredded cabbage, cilantro, and avocado, and break the freshly fried tortillas into your soup.

Easy Coconut Curry

Yield: 6 servings
Prep Time: 15 minutes
Cook Time: 25 to 35 minutes

4 tablespoons canola oil

1 large onion, diced

2-inch piece of ginger, peeled and minced

4 cloves garlic, minced

1 jalapeño or serrano, seeded and minced

2 tablespoons tomato paste

1 1/2 teaspoons ground coriander

1 1/2 teaspoons ground cumin

1/2 teaspoon turmeric

1 (14-ounce) block extra-firm tofu, or 1 pound chicken, cut into bite-sized pieces

1 head cauliflower, cut into florets

2 (14-ounce) cans coconut milk

1 1/2 teaspoons kosher salt

3/4 cup peas

FOR SERVING

Toasted cashews

Chopped cilantro

Lemon wedges

Basmati rice

Naan

TOOLS

Car Camping Base Kit

Large pot

Small skillet

My husband, Kismat, is from India and when we first started dating, he would bring me food that his mom made. I had never tried Indian food before I met him, and I was instantly hooked. I've since learned to cook Indian food, and we make it at our house often. It's a guaranteed way to get our kids to eat their veggies, and it makes us grown-ups happy too. This recipe is my take on a curry that's simple enough to cook outdoors. I like it with tofu, but chicken works too. Just add it in place of the tofu during cooking time. —*Aimee*

Heat the oil in a large pot over medium heat. Add the onion and sauté until softened and starting to caramelize, about 10 minutes. Stir in the ginger, garlic, and jalapeño, and sauté for another 2 minutes. Stir in the tomato paste, coriander, cumin, and turmeric, and cook until fragrant, about 1 minute. Add the tofu (or chicken) and cauliflower, stirring to coat with the spices. Stir in the coconut milk and salt, and bring the mixture to a boil. Reduce the heat to low and simmer for about 10 minutes, or until the cauliflower is tender. (If you're using chicken, simmer until it is cooked through, about 20 minutes.)

Meanwhile, in a dry skillet over low heat, toast the cashews until they're lightly browned, being careful not to burn them.

Stir the peas into the curry, cooking for another few minutes, until they're heated through. Season to taste with additional salt, if needed. Top with cashews, cilantro, and a squeeze of lemon wedges, and serve hot with basmati rice or naan.

EASY COCONUT CURRY

CHINESE SPAGHETTI (PG 132)

Chinese Spaghetti

Yield: 6 servings

Prep Time: 10 minutes

Cook Time: 25 to 30 minutes

3 to 4 tablespoons vegetable oil, divided

2 boneless, skinless chicken breasts

1 teaspoon kosher salt, plus more to taste

1/2 teaspoon freshly ground black pepper, plus more to taste

3 celery stalks, thinly sliced on the diagonal

1 yellow onion, halved and sliced

3 bunches baby bok choy, chopped

1 pound spaghetti

1/4 cup soy sauce

FOR SERVING

Chili-garlic sauce

TOOLS

Car Camping Base Kit

Large skillet

Large pot

Colander

This recipe is a total "mom recipe." Emily defined it best as "an Americanized version of an ethnic dish that is really easy to make, and secretly your favorite." My mom would make this for my brother and me when we were little, and for us, it was totally a Chinese dish because it contained soy sauce. I've added some bok choy to get some more greens into the mix, but its essence remains unchanged: a no-fuss, instantly committed-to-memory type of recipe that will surely become a staple in your arsenal. —Mai-Yan

In a large skillet, heat a tablespoon of the oil over medium-high heat. Add the chicken and season with a pinch of salt and pepper. Cook until chicken appears about halfway done through the thickest portion of the breast, about 5 to 8 minutes. Flip chicken breasts, season with a pinch more salt and pepper, and cook until the outside is golden brown and the meat is fully cooked, about another 8 to 10 minutes. Transfer chicken onto a cutting board. Set aside.

Return the skillet to medium-high heat and add the celery and onion. Cook for 5 to 7 minutes, stirring occasionally, until onions have softened but are still slightly crunchy. Stir in bok choy and cook for another 5 minutes. Turn off the heat and set aside.

Meanwhile, cook the spaghetti in a large pot of salted water, according to package directions.

Chop chicken into bite-sized pieces.

Carefully drain the water out of pasta pot, and return to low-medium heat. Add 1 tablespoon of the oil, soy sauce, and a pinch of black pepper, and mix well. Add prepared chicken and vegetables, and use tongs to mix everything together, making sure to pull the noodles apart from the center and capture any chicken and veggies hiding under the pile of pasta. (This a bit of an arm workout but worth it.) Season to taste with more salt and pepper, if needed. If the pasta seems dry, you can add a bit more oil. Serve with chili-garlic sauce.

Sweet and Spicy Scallion Crepes

Yield: 4 servings
Prep Time: 10 minutes
Cook Time: 15 minutes

FOR THE BATTER

1 cup chickpea flour

1 cup all-purpose flour

1/4 teaspoon kosher salt

2 1/4 cups water

1/2 cup vegetable oil

FOR THE FILLING

1/4 head of green cabbage, finely sliced (about 2 cups)

1 bunch of scallions, roughly chopped

2 teaspoons hoisin sauce, or more to taste per crepe

2 teaspoons chili-garlic sauce, or more to taste per crepe

TOOLS

Car Camping Base Kit

Large mixing bowl

Whisk

Bowls or jars for cabbage and scallions

9- or 10-inch cast iron or nonstick skillet

Aimee has the sweet tooth among us, while Emily and I are firmly in the savory camp, especially for breakfast. This recipe is our take on *jianbing*, a popular Chinese street breakfast slowly gaining popularity in the States. We're recommending it here for dinner. It is traditionally made with a paper-thin mung bean flour crepe, but we've substituted the mung bean flour with a chickpea and all-purpose flour blend to simplify ingredient sourcing. The batter yields a thin, springy crepe that is then slathered with hoisin and chili-garlic sauce. Raw cabbage brings some crunch and freshness to offset the sweet fire in your mouth. Rapid-fire cooking and creative folding will make you feel like you're on *Iron Chef America* while the tasty results will definitely leave you feeling like the winner. —*Mai-Yan*

AT HOME

In a large ziplock bag, combine chickpea flour, all-purpose flour, and the salt.

AT CAMP

Pour the flour-salt mixture into a large bowl and add the water. Whisk until there are no large lumps. Set aside.

Set out all filling ingredients (cabbage, scallions, hoisin, and chili-garlic sauce) so they are within reach of your cooking station. (Everything happens pretty fast with this dish so you need to be ready!)

Make the crepes: Heat 1 tablespoon of the oil in a skillet over medium-high heat. When the oil is hot, pour 1/3 cup of batter into the skillet, starting in the center and continuing out to make as big a circle as possible. Quickly spread out the batter even more, if possible, using your spatula. You are aiming for 8- to 9-inch crepes, no thicker than 1/8 inch. Immediately scatter a handful of chopped scallions on top of the batter. When the crepe edges look cooked and the center is semi-cooked, 1 to 2 minutes, fold the

crepe in half and spread about a teaspoon of hoisin sauce across the top of the folded half, followed by a teaspoon of chili-garlic sauce. Spread the sauces all the way to the edges.

Add chopped cabbage to half of the folded crepe and then fold in half one more time. You should have a crepe folded in quarters, or a rough triangle shape.

Serve immediately while still piping hot. Return to the skillet to make the next crepe, continuing the entire process until you run out of batter.

Buffalo Cauliflower Wraps

Yield: 4 servings
Prep Time: 20 minutes
Cook Time: 5 to 7 minutes

FOR THE PICKLED ONIONS

1 small red onion, thinly sliced

¼ cup white vinegar

¼ teaspoon sugar

¼ teaspoon kosher salt

FOR THE CAULIFLOWER

1 large head cauliflower, cut into florets

4 tablespoons vegetable oil

½ teaspoon kosher salt

¼ to ½ cup hot sauce, such as Frank's Red Hot

FOR THE SCALLION CREAM CHEESE

½ cup cream cheese

2 tablespoons thinly sliced scallions

FOR THE WRAPS

4 (12-inch) spinach or plain tortilla wraps

4 leaves romaine lettuce

Salt and vinegar potato chips

TOOLS

Car Camping Base Kit

Usually I find wraps boring, but these are anything but. They're stuffed with spicy cauliflower, pickled onions, cream cheese, and the kicker—salt and vinegar potato chips! The cauliflower cooks quickly in foil packets and then it's just a matter of putting everything together. If you don't have a campfire, you can skip wrapping the cauliflower in foil and sauté the florets in a pan on a camp stove instead. —*Aimee*

AT HOME

Make the pickled onions: Combine the onion, vinegar, sugar, and salt in a jar. Seal it tightly, label it, and keep chilled until ready to use. (You can also prepare this at camp, but make sure to do it at least an hour before you're going to eat, to give the onions some time to pickle.)

AT CAMP

First prepare the cauliflower: Cut 4 pieces of aluminum foil large enough to create a foil pouch around about one-fourth of the florets. Divide the florets between the pieces of foil. Drizzle with the oil and sprinkle with the salt. Fold the aluminum foil into a pouch (see the Appendix for instructions), and place on a grate set over a campfire.

Cook until the cauliflower is just tender, about 4 to 5 minutes, then remove from heat and pour about 1 to 2 tablespoons of hot sauce on top of the cauliflower in each pouch.

While the cauliflower is cooking, make the scallion cream cheese: In a small bowl, combine the cream cheese with the scallions, mashing in the scallions with a fork.

On the campfire grate (or in a large skillet on your stove), warm the tortillas. Spread each tortilla with about 2 tablespoons of cream cheese mixture followed by a romaine leaf, the contents of one foil packet of cauliflower, and a handful each of the pickled onions and the chips. Wrap tightly like a burrito and serve.

Sausage Mac and Cheese

Yield: 4 servings (8 servings as a side)

Prep Time: 15 minutes

Cook Time: 30 minutes

2 cups shredded sharp cheddar

1 cup shredded Parmesan

1 pound pasta shells

4 tablespoons butter, divided

2 cups milk

1 large yellow onion, finely chopped

2 tablespoons all-purpose flour

1 cup Guinness beer, or other dark ale

1 teaspoon dry mustard

1 teaspoon kosher salt, plus more to taste

½ teaspoon freshly ground black pepper, plus more to taste

4 spicy pre-cooked sausages, sliced crosswise (andouille or spicy Italian are good)

TOOLS

Car Camping Base Kit

Large pot

Large mixing bowl

Small pot

Whisk

Beer. Cheese. Butter. Spicy Sausage. Pasta. *Boom!* The inspiration for this recipe came from a dinner at Crossroads Cafe in Joshua Tree where I had ordered a soup with a side of mac & cheese. When the soup arrived I realized it was more cheese sauce than soup, with pieces of sausage held hostage mid-bowl, so I decided to pour it over my mac & cheese. Here's our version of this sinful pairing. Even if Guinness isn't your favorite beer, it gives the sauce great depth and a rich flavor that's worth the splurge. —*Mai-Yan*

AT HOME

Place the shredded cheddar and Parmesan cheeses in a large zip-lock bag and keep cool.

AT CAMP

In a large pot full of salted water over high heat, cook the pasta according to the package directions, just until al dente. Drain and transfer the pasta to a large bowl. Add 1 tablespoon of the butter, mix well, and set aside.

Meanwhile, in a small pot over low heat, heat the milk. The intent is to have warm milk ready for the cheese sauce. (If you skip this step, you will likely end up with a "broken sauce," where fats and liquids separate creating little lumps floating in a watery base. In short, don't skip this!)

Set the large pot you cooked the pasta in over medium heat, and add the remaining three tablespoons of butter and the onions. Cook the onion until it is translucent and soft, about 5 to 8 minutes. Add the flour and mix well. Let the mixture cook for 5 minutes, stirring occasionally.

Slowly (important!) whisk the warmed milk into the pot, followed by the beer. Bring the mixture to a boil and then reduce the heat to low, whisking continuously until the sauce is thickened. Add the mustard, salt, and pepper. Stir in the cheese in small batches as it melts into the sauce. Adjust seasoning with salt and pepper, going a little on the salty side. Add pasta and sausage to the sauce and stir well. Serve piping hot.

Sweet Potato Chipotle Flautas

Yield: 8 flautas / 4 servings

Prep Time: 15 minutes

Cook Time: 25 minutes

2 medium sweet potatoes

1 (14-ounce) can black beans

2 tablespoons sour cream

1 tablespoon chipotles in adobo, minced

Juice of 1 lime

1 teaspoon kosher salt

8 (10-inch) soft flour tortillas

2 tablespoons vegetable oil, divided

FOR SERVING

Additional sour cream

TOOLS

Car Camping Base Kit

Large mixing bowl

Large skillet

Flautas are one of my favorite foods, but it is rare to find any that are vegetarian. I have played with many different combinations to try and get something that appeals to everyone in my camping crew, and this is the clear winner. They are simple to fry up at camp, and actually work well as a second-day lunchtime treat, even at room temperature. We once brought them to a picnic at the Hollywood Bowl. This may not sound very outdoorsy, but the bowl has quite a bit of rustic green space meant for pre-concert picnicking. The weather that late-summer evening was perfect as we picnicked and drank wine under the trees. —*Emily*

Cut two pieces of aluminum foil large enough to fully wrap around each sweet potato. Wrap the potatoes in the aluminum foil and set them on the grate of the campfire. Cook until soft, about 20 minutes. (The time it takes to cook depends on where you place them in the fire, so check on them after about 10 minutes and adjust the position in the fire as needed.) Remove from fire and set aside. When the potatoes are cool enough to handle, remove the aluminum foil and slice in half. Scoop the potato flesh into a large bowl, eating or discarding the skin. Add the undrained black beans, sour cream, chipotles, lime juice, and salt. Mix well.

Lay out the first tortilla and place about 3 tablespoons of the potato mixture down the center, spreading the mixture all the way to the edges of the tortilla. Tightly roll the tortilla and set aside with the edge facing down to hold it together. Repeat for each tortilla.

In a skillet, heat one tablespoon of the oil over medium-high heat. Place 3 to 4 prepared tortillas into the oil, seam-side down. Fry until golden brown on the bottom, about 2 minutes. Using tongs, gently roll the tortillas, cooking until all sides are golden brown. Remove from heat and transfer cooked flautas onto a paper towel. Repeat until all flautas are cooked.

Serve with additional sour cream on the side.

Skillet Vegetable Lasagna

Yield: 6 servings

Prep Time: 10 minutes

Cook Time: 20 to 25 minutes

2 tablespoons extra-virgin olive oil

1 medium zucchini, diced

1 red bell pepper, diced

½ teaspoon kosher salt

6 cups marinara sauce

8 ounces lasagna noodles

6 ounces baby spinach

8 ounces ricotta

TOOLS

Car Camping Base Kit

10- to 12-inch, high-sided skillet with a lid

One of my favorite things about camping is the "campfire talk." I live for deep, winding conversations (hence, my double major in biology and philosophy), and so my family often defers topics "to the campfire" when I start down the rabbit hole at home. These nights need a meal that is easy to execute without a lot of prep, like this delicious lasagna. Its simplicity lets you focus on the camping experience and get right into the good stuff. —*Emily*

In a deep skillet, heat the oil over medium heat. Add the zucchini, bell pepper, and salt, and sauté until the vegetables soften and begin to brown, about 5 minutes. Transfer the vegetables to a cutting board or bowl, and set aside, leaving the remaining oil in the skillet.

Remove the skillet from the heat, and pour about 1½ cups of the marinara sauce into the bottom of the skillet. Then layer in ⅓ of the lasagna noodles, followed by ⅓ of the zucchini–bell pepper mixture, ⅓ of the spinach, and ⅓ of the ricotta. Repeat in that order, adding two more layers, and ending with a fourth and final layer of pasta, marinara, and ricotta. Cover.

Over low heat, cook for about 20 minutes, or until the noodles are soft and the lasagna is heated through. (You'll probably need to stick a fork in the lasagna to make sure the pasta is cooked through.) Remove from the heat and let sit for about 5 minutes before serving.

SWEET POTATO CHIPOTLE FLAUTAS (PG 140)

SKILLET VEGETABLE LASAGNA (PG 141)

BARBEQUE RANCH SALAD FLATBREAD (PG 144)

CHILI GRILLED CHEESE SANDWICH (PG 145)

Barbeque Ranch Salad Flatbread

Yield: 4 servings
Prep Time: 20 minutes
Cook Time: 20 minutes

FOR THE FLATBREAD

1 pound premade pizza dough

2 tablespoons extra-virgin olive oil

4 cloves garlic, minced

1/4 cup all-purpose flour

FOR THE SALAD

1 to 2 tablespoons extra-virgin olive oil

2 boneless, skinless chicken breasts, sliced into 1/2-inch cutlets or pounded into 1/2-inch thick pieces

1/2 teaspoon kosher salt

1/2 teaspoon freshly ground black pepper

1 large head romaine lettuce, torn into bite-sized pieces

2 carrots, shredded

2 scallions, chopped

1/2 cup croutons

FOR SERVING

Ranch dressing

Barbeque sauce

TOOLS

Car Camping Base Kit

Large cast iron or nonstick skillet

Large mixing bowl

Silicone mat, extra large cutting board, or other clean work surface

Rolling pin or clean bottle to use as a rolling pin

Being Dirty Gourmet, we can never get away with not cooking for everyone when we're outdoors. This recipe is a good one to have in your back pocket for lazy days surrounded by hungry people. As long as you've got pizza dough in the freezer, you have the basis for a hearty and speedy meal. If you need a little extra bulk, add black beans and corn to the mix. —*Emily*

First prepare the chicken: Heat a tablespoon of the oil in a large skillet over high heat. Season the chicken with salt and pepper and place in the skillet. Cook for 2 to 3 minutes, then turn. Continue cooking until the chicken is no longer pink inside. Remove from heat and set aside. When cool enough to handle, chop into bite-sized pieces.

Next prepare the salad: In a large bowl, combine the lettuce, carrots, and scallions. Set aside.

Divide the pizza dough into four balls. On a clean surface, roll out the first ball into an 8-inch round, using flour as needed to prevent the dough from sticking to the surface or rolling pin.

In the same skillet used for the chicken over medium heat, heat 1 tablespoon of the oil. Add half of the garlic to the oil and carefully add one dough-round to the skillet. Cook for about 3 to 5 minutes keeping a close eye on the heat so the dough doesn't burn.

Flip the dough when it's golden brown and continue cooking until the second side is browned. Set aside under a towel to keep warm while you're cooking the rest of the flatbreads. Add additional oil to the pan as needed to cook the remaining flatbreads.

Toss the salad with the chicken, croutons, and some ranch dressing. Divide the salad between the flatbreads and drizzle with barbeque sauce and more ranch dressing to taste. Cut in quarters, or eat folded like a taco.

Chili Grilled Cheese Sandwich

Yield: 1 serving

Prep Time: 10 minutes

Cook Time: About 5 minutes

Spray oil

2 slices sourdough bread

4 tablespoons shredded sharp cheddar cheese, divided

3 to 4 tablespoons of chili

Pickled jalapeños and carrots, to taste

TOOLS

Car Camping Base Kit

Cast iron pie iron

Heatproof gloves

As far as sandwiches go, grilled cheese is hard to beat. Although I still have a soft spot for the grilled American cheese sandwiches of my childhood, this recipe is its natural evolution. Since chili is usually topped with cheese, putting it inside a grilled cheese sandwich is a no-brainer. We added a little spice and contrast with the pickled jalapeños, because we like everything spicy, but you can safely skip this ingredient without compromising the amazingness of this sandwich. —*Mai-Yan*

Preheat the pie iron either directly over the flames of the stove or the coals of a campfire for about 2 minutes on each side.

Open up the pie iron (be careful—the hook and metal rods get hot) and set it down on a heatproof surface. Spray both sides of the iron with a layer of oil. Put one slice of bread in one of the pie iron halves. (Don't worry about the bread not quite fitting into the shape. It's actually better if the bread is a little larger than the pie iron.) Add 2 tablespoons of the cheese, followed by the chili. Add the jalapeños and carrots to taste. Top the lot with the remaining 2 tablespoons of cheese and cover with a second slice of bread. Carefully close the pie iron, forcing it down over any bread that is spilling out. Use a knife to trim the excess bread, if needed.

Place the pie iron directly over flames or coals for 2 minutes on each side. (Times will vary depending on how hot your fire is.) Your chili grilled cheese is ready when the bread is golden brown with charred edges. Return pie iron to a heatproof surface, release the sandwich, and cut in half. Serve immediately.

Steak and Veggie Skewers with Harissa

Yield: 4 skewers

Prep Time: 15 minutes at home, 10 minutes at camp

Cook Time: 20 minutes

FOR THE SKEWERS

1 pound ribeye steak

1/4 cup extra-virgin olive oil

2 cloves garlic, finely chopped

2 tablespoons fresh Italian parsley, finely chopped

Juice of 1 medium lemon

1/2 teaspoon kosher salt

1/2 teaspoon freshly ground black pepper

1 sweet onion, cut into chunks

1 red bell pepper, cut into chunks

FOR THE HARISSA

1 teaspoon red chile flakes

1/2 teaspoon ground coriander

1/2 teaspoon ground cumin

1/2 teaspoon caraway seeds

1 red bell pepper

2 tablespoons extra-virgin olive oil

1 small red onion, chopped

3 cloves garlic, chopped

1 1/2 teaspoons tomato paste

Juice of 1 medium lemon

1/2 teaspoon kosher salt

TOOLS

Car Camping Base Kit

10-inch cast iron skillet

Small mixing bowl

4 (12-inch) skewer sticks

Heatproof gloves

There's something extremely satisfying about hearing the hiss of food hit a hot grill. These skewers provide just that. This simple but classic grilling recipe is one that we like to serve with Dutch Oven Jeweled Rice (see Car Camping, Side Dishes). The marinade itself is pretty straightforward, but what really brings this whole meal together is the homemade harissa sauce. We suggest making it ahead of dinnertime so you can focus on grilling and serve the skewers piping hot. Because these are cooked right on the firepit's grate, you'll be at the mercy of the last occupant who may or may not have cleaned off the grate after using it. You can clean off a dirty grate by balling up some foil, grabbing it with your tongs, and using it as an abrasive to scrape off any unidentified leftover bits. —Mai-Yan

AT HOME

Trim any fat off the steak and cut meat into 1-inch cubes. Place into a gallon-size ziplock bag.

In a small bowl, whisk together oil, garlic, parsley, lemon juice, salt, and pepper. Add the marinade to the cubed steak and seal the bag. Massage contents so the steak is evenly coated. Keep chilled until you are ready to grill.

For the harissa, combine the chile flakes, coriander, cumin, and caraway seeds. Package and store with other non-perishables coming on your trip.

AT CAMP

First make the harissa: Place the bell pepper on a grate over a hot fire. With tongs, rotate constantly until blackened, about 5 minutes. Peel and chop finely. Set aside.

In a dry skillet, toast the spice mix over medium heat for a few minutes. Add the oil and onion, and cook until caramelized, about 10 minutes. Add the garlic and tomato paste, and stir for another minute. Add the roasted pepper and mash the mixture with a potato masher or a fork until it's as smooth as possible. Stir in the lemon juice and salt. Set aside or transfer to a small bowl.

Adjust the fire so there are flames directly under the grate. You're going for medium flames licking the underside of the grate.

Thread steak, onion, and bell pepper onto skewers, leaving a little room in between the ingredients. Spray the grate with oil and place skewers directly on the grate. Hopefully, you get a satisfying sizzle as soon as they land. Cook for 2 to 3 minutes and then rotate a quarter turn. Keep cooking for another 2 minutes per 4 "sides." Check if meat is cooked to *your* liking but we recommend serving them at medium temperature with a little pink still showing in the middle.

Smother with harissa sauce and serve with a side of Dutch Oven Jeweled Rice.

Cornbread Chili Pie

Yield: 6 to 8 servings

Prep Time: 20 minutes

Cook Time: 1 hour

12 ounces ground beef

3 medium onions, chopped

4 garlic cloves, chopped

2 tablespoons chipotles in adobo, minced

4 tablespoons chili powder

2 tablespoons cumin

1 tablespoon oregano

2 teaspoons kosher salt

2 (28-ounce) cans diced tomatoes

3 (14-ounce) cans pinto beans

1 cup water

2 tablespoons molasses

FOR THE CORNBREAD

1 cup all-purpose flour

1 cup cornmeal

¼ cup sugar

4 teaspoons baking powder

¾ teaspoon kosher salt

1 cup milk

¼ cup extra-virgin olive oil

FOR SERVING

Diced avocado

Lime wedges

Chopped onion

Shredded cheddar cheese

TOOLS

Car Camping Base Kit

12-inch Dutch oven

Heatproof gloves or lid lifter

Chili highlights all of the benefits of a cast iron pot: slow, even heating and the ability to utilize the campfire to help build the smoky flavor. I've been working on perfecting my chili recipe for years. There are so many different ways you can go with it, and it always leads to a lively discussion with other chili enthusiasts. Are beans acceptable? Do you need fancy ground chiles or is regular ol' chili powder just fine? Should you add molasses, coffee, chocolate, cinnamon, dry mustard, or beer? This is my final version (for now). It balances some classic flavors with ease and practicality in order to prepare it at the campground. And the cornbread goes right on top—one of those one-pot meals that just gets better as you sit together around the campfire. —*Emily*

AT HOME

Prepare the dry ingredients for the cornbread topping: In a ziplock bag, combine the flour, cornmeal, sugar, baking powder, and salt.

AT CAMP

Place a 12-inch Dutch oven on a grate set over a campfire. When the Dutch oven is hot, add the ground beef and onions and cook until the beef is browned and the onions are translucent, about 10 minutes. Add the garlic and chipotles, and cook until garlic is fragrant, about 2 minutes. Add the chili powder, cumin, oregano, and salt. Cook for 1 minute longer, until fragrant. Add the tomatoes, pinto beans with their juice, water, and molasses. Bring to a boil, cover, and then adjust the coals so that the chili can simmer for about 30 minutes.

Meanwhile, make the cornbread. Add the milk and oil into the ziplock bag of dry ingredients (or use a bowl), and squish (or stir) to combine wet and dry ingredients.

Taste the chili and season with additional salt or chipotle as needed. Squeeze or scoop the cornbread mixture over the top of the chili, being careful not to splash it. Cover and add 21 coals to the top of the lid (which should get you to about 425°F). Bake until cornbread is brown on top and a knife inserted in the center of the cornbread comes out clean, about 20 minutes.

Serve with avocado, limes, chopped onion, and shredded cheese.

cornbread Add 1/4 C o.o.↓ 1 c milk

Dutch Oven Chicken Pot Pie

Yield: 6 servings

Prep Time: 20 minutes

Cook Time: 45 to 60 minutes

2 tablespoons vegetable oil

1 yellow onion, chopped

2 chicken breasts, cubed

Kosher salt and freshly ground black pepper, to taste

1 1/2 cups diced carrots

1 1/2 cups diced potatoes

1 cup diced celery

1 cup peas

3 garlic cloves, minced

4 cups chicken or vegetable broth

1 teaspoon herbes de Provence

4 tablespoons of water

2 tablespoons cornstarch

1 sheet of frozen puff pastry, defrosted

TOOLS

Car Camping Base Kit

10-inch Dutch oven

Heatproof gloves

Lid lifter

Small mixing bowl

Pot pie is one of my mom's specialties that she cooked for us as kids, and we love to take these traditional types of recipes and modify them for the campfire. This is a good recipe to start just before the coals are ready in your fire. The method begins with active cooking over the flames on a grate and then moves into the fire bed with coals to bake the puff pastry lid. —*Emily*

Preheat the Dutch oven and lid for 10 minutes by placing on the grate over some flames. (Ideally, the flames are licking the cast iron, rather than engulfing it.) Add the oil. Add the onion and chicken, and stir together. (If the Dutch oven has been preheated properly, you will get a satisfying sizzling sound immediately.) Season with a pinch of salt and pepper. Cook until onions are translucent and chicken looks mostly done, stirring occasionally, about 5 to 10 minutes.

Add the carrots, potatoes, celery, peas, and garlic along with another pinch of salt and pepper, and mix well. Add the broth and herbes de Provence and stir. Make sure there's enough heat under the grate to keep a simmer going. Cover and simmer for about 10 minutes, checking in to see if the potatoes are starting to soften. It's OK if they are still a little firm.

Meanwhile, in a small bowl, mix the water and cornstarch together until thoroughly mixed.

Add the cornstarch slurry to the Dutch oven and stir well. Remove the Dutch oven from the direct heat and adjust seasoning to taste. (Make sure you have a nice bed of coals ready for the next step, adjusting your fire location as needed.)

Place puff pastry on top of pot pie filling, covering it entirely and folding over any edges that don't fit. Cover with lid and place Dutch oven in the coal bed with about 8 coals on the bottom and 17 on the lid. Bake for 20 to 30 minutes, rotating Dutch oven and lid in opposite directions every 10 minutes or so. Check the pot pie after the first 10 minutes to make sure it's cooking evenly. It is done when the puff pastry has expanded and is golden brown.

Campfire Bibimbap

Yield: 6 to 8 servings

Prep Time: 10 minutes

Cook Time: 20 minutes

3 cups medium grain rice

4 cups water

2 cups sliced mushrooms

2 cups spinach, roughly chopped

1 cup bean sprouts

1 cup kimchi

1 cup julienned carrots

FOR THE MUSHROOMS

¼ cup soy sauce

2 tablespoons rice vinegar

4 teaspoons brown sugar

FOR THE CHILI SAUCE

¼ cup gochujang

1 tablespoon plus 1 teaspoon brown sugar

1 tablespoon sesame seeds

1 tablespoon rice vinegar

2 teaspoons sesame oil

2 teaspoons soy sauce

FOR SERVING

Sesame seeds

TOOLS

Car Camping Base Kit

12-inch Dutch oven

Lid lifter

10-inch cast iron skillet

Small mixing bowl

Heatproof gloves

We are excited about how popular our national parks are these days, especially since that means more people falling in love with the outdoors. On the other hand, it's become really difficult to a get a campsite. So we've gotten into the habit of reserving sites, sometimes up to six months in advance. A lot of times we'll forget about our reservations and suddenly realize there's a "surprise planned" camping trip. Not complaining about that part!

On one of these trips, we experimented with a paella recipe, and discovered how effective Dutch ovens are for cooking rice. That got us thinking about *bibimbap*, a Korean rice dish cooked in a hot stone pot that creates a glorious layer of crispy rice at the bottom. The rice is then topped with a variety of fresh and cooked ingredients, and then tossed with *gochujang*, an addictive sweet and spicy fermented chili sauce.

The hotter the fire, the faster the rice will cook, so load up the lid with as many coals as will fit in one layer. If you can get the water to a boil, you will be rewarded with fluffier rice. If you don't, the rice will still cook, but it may turn out a little softer and stickier. —*Mai-Yan*

AT HOME

Prepare the mushroom sauce: In a small leakproof container, combine soy sauce, rice vinegar, and brown sugar.

Prepare the chili sauce: In a small leakproof container, combine gochujang, brown sugar, sesame seeds, rice vinegar, sesame oil, and soy sauce.

AT CAMP

In the Dutch oven, mix rice and water together. Place the Dutch oven over a bed of about 10 coals and cover. Place about 14 to 18 coals on top of the lid. Cook until rice has absorbed the water, about 15 to 20 minutes. Check on the rice after 10 minutes, and then every 5 minutes until cooked through. When done, remove the lid and place the Dutch oven on the grate of the campfire over medium heat.

Meanwhile, add the mushrooms to a cast iron skillet on the grate of the campfire. Add the prepared mushroom sauce, stirring occasionally until the mushrooms have absorbed all the liquid. Set aside.

Directly into the Dutch oven, spoon the mushrooms, spinach, bean sprouts, kimchi, and carrots into piles around the top of the rice. Pour the prepared chili sauce in the center of it all. Garnish with sesame seeds.

Gather everyone around to *ooh and ah* at the beauty, and then stir the whole thing together.

Serve (or eat) straight from the Dutch oven, scraping the bottom each time to include some crispy rice in each serving. Keep the Dutch oven heating on the grate so that second servings will have even more crispy rice.

Campfire Pizza

Yield: 2 10-inch pizzas
Prep Time: 15 minutes
Cook Time: 20 minutes

1 pound premade pizza dough

2 tablespoons extra-virgin olive oil, divided

½ cup pizza sauce (optional)

1 cup shredded mozzarella

1 cup cherry tomatoes, halved

10 leaves fresh basil, sliced

Sea salt, to taste

TOOLS

10- or 12-inch Dutch oven

Clean surface for rolling dough

Lid lifter

Heatproof gloves

I'd only dabbled in bread baking until a couple of years ago when I picked up a book called *Josey Baker Bread* and became obsessed with making sourdough bread. And his pizza recipe and method deliver out-of-this-world results: You first cook the pizza on the stovetop in a skillet and then finish it off in the broiler. We modified it for a campfire and it turned out great; we've been doing it this way ever since. Of course using Josey Baker's dough recipe is best, but this method elevates even the store-bought stuff. To avoid burning the bottom of your pie, prep and set out all of the ingredients near the campfire before you start assembling. —*Aimee*

Since you'll be making multiple pizzas quickly, use a few large chunks of charcoal rather than a bunch of smaller ones. These will hold their heat longer and be easier to remove and replace multiple times.

Preheat the Dutch oven by setting it on a grate over your campfire.

While the Dutch oven is getting hot, divide the pizza dough into two equal pieces. On a clean work surface, stretch or roll each piece into a circle approximately the size of the Dutch oven bottom.

Set out all of the toppings: pizza sauce, mozzarella, tomatoes, basil, and salt.

Once the Dutch oven is hot, add a tablespoon of olive oil. The oil should smoke right away. Carefully set one dough round onto the bottom of the Dutch oven. Onto the dough, spread about half of the pizza sauce, then sprinkle with half the mozzarella, half the cherry tomato halves, and half the basil. Season with a little salt, especially around the crust. Using a spatula, lift up the dough to check the bottom. Once it's lightly browned, about 5 minutes, cover the Dutch oven and move it to a cooler part of the grate or directly in the fire pit, with no coals on the bottom.

The bottom of your pizza is essentially done at this stage—the goal now is to get the top to brown. Place about 20 coals on the lid, or as many that will fit. Check on the pizza every 2 minutes until the top is lightly browned. Using a spatula, carefully remove the pizza from the Dutch oven. Repeat to cook the second pizza.

DRINKS

Blackberry Mulled Wine

Yield: 4 servings
Prep Time: 5 minutes
Cook Time: 15 minutes

¼ cup sugar

2 cinnamon sticks

4 green cardamom pods, lightly crushed

1 orange

1 cup blackberries

1 (750 ml) bottle of red wine

1 teaspoon vanilla extract

TOOLS

Car Camping Base Kit
Vegetable peeler
Medium pot
Ladle

One of my favorite childhood memories is a road trip with my family to Northern California. We drove all the way to Crescent City from LA, camping along the way. We hiked through the redwoods and swam in the Russian River, but the stand-out part of the trip was picking and eating the blackberries that grew all over one of the campgrounds we stayed at. It was my mom's birthday, and since we were surrounded by wild blackberries, my dad made her blackberry cobbler with vanilla ice cream, followed by pancakes with blackberries and melted ice cream for breakfast the next morning.

I always have blackberries in the house, and this Blackberry Mulled Wine recipe came to be one evening when I realized I had a handful that were on their way out. The tart blackberries balance the sweet spices and vanilla, and it's just the thing for a cool night outside. —*Aimee*

AT HOME

Combine sugar, cinnamon sticks, and cardamom in a small container.

AT CAMP

Using a vegetable peeler, peel the zest in wide strips from half of the orange. Cut the orange in half and juice it directly into a medium pot. Add the zest, blackberries, and sugar mixture and, using a fork or the back of your wooden spoon, muddle the mixture just a little bit. Add the wine, cover, and bring the mixture to a simmer over high heat. Reduce the heat to low and simmer for about 10 minutes. Remove from heat and discard the cinnamon, cardamom, and orange peel.

Stir in the vanilla, and ladle into cups to serve.

Canelazo

Yield: 6 servings

Prep Time: 5 minutes

Cook Time: 25 minutes

½ cup sugar

6 cinnamon sticks

4 cups water

2 cups fresh-squeezed orange juice

6 ounces cachaça or white rum

TOOLS

Car Camping Base Kit

Medium pot

Ladle

Best described as a cross between a hot toddy and mulled wine, this Ecuadorian hot drink is delicious, fruity, and spiced with cinnamon. I discovered it while on a trip to the Galapagos, where I got to snorkel with sea turtles, reef sharks, and penguins—a once in a lifetime trip! Despite being at the Equator, the water was quite chilly and *canelazo* was just the thing to warm up my bones. It is typically made with *aguardiente*, a sugarcane-based liquor, and a local fruit called *naranjilla*. These ingredients are difficult to find outside of South America, so we've adapted our version to use either cachaça or rum with fresh orange juice. The important thing when making this drink is to let the ingredients simmer, as indicated, so it becomes nice and thick with a lot of cinnamon flavor. *Salud! —Mai-Yan*

AT HOME

Measure out the sugar and place the cinnamon sticks in a small container.

AT CAMP

Put water, juice, sugar, and cinnamon sticks in a medium pot and bring to a boil over high heat. Lower the heat and simmer for 20 minutes to fully extract the flavor from the cinnamon sticks.

Ladle about one cup of the liquid into each mug, adding 1 ounce of cachaça per drink.

Serve hot with an optional swizzle cinnamon stick.

Pineapple Sake Cooler

Yield: 4 servings

Prep Time: 10 minutes

2½ cups pineapple juice

1½ cups sake

Juice from 4 small limes (about ¼ cup)

1 jalapeño, seeded and sliced

2 limes, sliced

1 cup mint leaves, roughly chopped

4 cups ice

TOOLS

Car Camping Base Kit

1 (32-ounce) reusable water bottle

4 (16-ounce) Mason jars

I'm not ashamed to say that one of the best things about car camping is daytime drinking. Once the madness of planning, packing, and setting up camp is done, it's time to relax! This Pineapple Sake Cooler is a refreshing cocktail for hot days when ice is still aplenty in your cooler. (If you keep ice in the bag it comes in rather than pouring it into your cooler, it lasts longer and you'll have clean ice to put into your drinks.) Sake is Japanese rice wine with an alcohol content similar to wine made from grapes. Paired with a lot of fresh lime juice, mint, pineapple juice—and great company—this summer cooler gets the afternoon started just right. —*Mai-Yan*

Into a water bottle, combine pineapple juice, sake, and lime juice. Shake to mix.

Into each jar, place 2 to 3 jalapeño slices and 4 lime slices. Divide the chopped mint between the jars. Use a spoon to muddle the ingredients in each jar to extract the natural oils and juices from the ingredients. Top up each jar with ice and pour in juice-sake mixture. Stir from the bottom so all the ingredients are distributed throughout the jar. Top each jar with a slice of lime and serve.

Micheladas

Yield: 4 servings

Prep Time: 5 minutes

½ teaspoon chili powder

1 tablespoon kosher salt

1 lime, quartered

4 cups ice

1½ cups bloody Mary mix
(12 ounces), divided

2 teaspoons freshly ground black
pepper, divided

Worcestershire and Tabasco sauce

2 light Mexican beers

4 slices jalapeño

TOOLS

Car Camping Base Kit

4 tall glasses

A Michelada is essentially a beer cocktail so it's nice and light, which is good for warm days full of outdoor play. Experiment with different variations of this popular drink, but don't budge on the spice level. —*Emily*

On a small plate, mix the chili powder and salt.

Rub the rims of the glasses with lime and then squeeze the remaining lime juice into each glass. Fill glasses with ice, then to each glass add 3 ounces of bloody Mary mix, ½ teaspoon pepper, a dash of Worcestershire, and a dash of Tabasco. Divide the beer between the glasses. Top with jalapeño slices and serve.

Mason Jar Sangria

Yield: 4 to 6 servings

Prep Time: 5 minutes

1 (750 ml) bottle dry Spanish red wine

Juice of 1 large grapefruit (about 1 cup)

Juice of 2 limes (about $\frac{1}{8}$ cup)

$\frac{1}{4}$ cup sugar

1 orange, sliced into small pieces

1 apple, cored and chopped into bite-sized pieces

1 cup grapes

1 lime, sliced into small pieces

Ice

TOOLS

Car Camping Base Kit

Large pitcher

4 to 6 (16-ounce) Mason jars

This refreshing sangria is a popular beach drink. You can make it at home or at camp, and stash the individual-sized jars in your cooler to drink later. The fruit soaks up the wine and starts to taste a little boozy, yet with the ice and all the fruit, it's not too high in alcohol. I like to make a virgin version for the kids, with juice, sparkling water, and fruit. —*Aimee*

In a large pitcher, combine the wine, grapefruit juice, lime juice, and sugar. Stir to combine.

In a medium bowl, combine the orange, apple, grapes, and lime. Divide the fruit mixture evenly among the jars, then add the wine mixture. You can fill the jars half to three-quarters full, depending on how much ice you like. Cover the jars with the lids and screw on the rings to close. Keep the sangria cold in your cooler until serving time.

To serve, fill jars with ice.

DESSERTS

Skillet Apple Pie with Cognac Butter

Yield: 4 to 6 servings
Prep Time: 10 minutes
Cook Time: 45 minutes

8 Granny Smith apples, cored and thinly sliced

¼ cup sugar

Juice of 1 small lemon

1 frozen pie crust, thawed

1 tablespoon brown sugar

FOR THE COGNAC BUTTER

4 tablespoons salted butter, softened

1 tablespoon cognac

1 tablespoon brown sugar

TOOLS

Car Camping Base Kit

12-inch cast iron skillet

12-inch Dutch oven lid

Heatproof gloves or lid lifter

Even though my dad's main drink is Miller Lite (thanks to his favorite racecar driver), he's always loved cognac. I love the duality of watching him chase the fancy cognac with his light beer—this describes his personality well. It also reminds me of the duality of "Dirty Gourmet."

I once saw a dessert similar to this one served in a cast iron skillet. The waiter poured something over the top that sizzled and smelled incredible. I assumed it was brandy butter, and planned to create that, but when this recipe came to be, we used my dad's cognac instead. The pie was very easy to make and delicious to eat, and the cognac butter was a smooth finish. —*Emily*

Place the apples in a cast iron skillet. Sprinkle with the sugar and lemon juice, and cover with the thawed pie crust. Try to get it evenly distributed across the top, but don't worry too much if it is uneven, or unevenly thawed. Sprinkle the top of the crust with the brown sugar. Cover with a lid.

Place the skillet on the grate of a campfire over medium heat. Add approximately 14 coals on top of the lid.

Meanwhile, prepare the cognac butter. In a bowl, add the butter, then stir in the cognac and brown sugar. Set aside.

Check the pie after 10 minutes. If it is burning along the edges, reduce the heat underneath by adjusting the campfire. Or remove the skillet from the grate and continue to bake using only the coals on top. Cook for approximately 30 more minutes, or until the crust is crispy and golden brown. Scoop the cognac butter onto the center of the pie while it's still hot, letting it melt all over the top.

Olive Oil Orange Cakes

Yield: 6 cakes
Prep Time: 30 minutes
Cook Time: 10 to 15 minutes

1¼ cups all-purpose flour
³⁄₄ cup sugar
1 teaspoon baking powder
½ teaspoon kosher salt
2 eggs
Zest of 1 orange
6 oranges
6 tablespoons extra-virgin olive oil
1 teaspoon vanilla extract

TOOLS

Car Camping Base Kit
Vegetable peeler or zester

There's a classic campfire dessert recipe for making brownies in orange peel cups. Despite not being a baker, I decided to try it. I was not impressed. The most disturbing part of the process was the pulpy orange soup aftermath created by scooping the fruit out of the orange peels. However, using an orange peel as a baking vessel remained in my mind as a good idea, so I decided to try it again while resolving the orange soup problem at the same time.

Olive oil cake showcases the orange flavor well, and the orange coring instructions will leave you with intact oranges that you can actually snack on. For the win!

Baking with the campfire can be tricky, but this recipe is pretty forgiving with the orange peel acting as a thick heat barrier. You'll want to keep a close eye on these once they are in the fire, but don't worry too much if the peel gets charred on the outside. —*Mai-Yan*

AT HOME

Combine flour, sugar, baking powder, and salt in a gallon-size ziplock bag. Seal well.

Crack the eggs into a jar, and pack in your cooler.

AT CAMP

Zest the orange and add zest to the flour mixture bag.

Prepare the oranges: Using a sharp paring knife, make a peel-deep cut around the navel of the orange. Pull navel out, leaving a little hole in the top of the orange. Make 6 shallow peel-deep vertical cuts down the side of the orange, stopping halfway at the widest part of the orange. Carefully pry open the top of the orange peel petals you just created, and slide a spoon between the peel and the fruit of the orange. Slowly move the spoon around the entire perimeter of the orange to separate it from the peel. Pull the fruit out from the peel and set aside for snacking. You should be left with a hollowed-out orange cup, which will become your baking vessel. Repeat for each orange and set aside.

Now make the batter. Into the flour mixture ziplock bag, add the eggs, olive oil, and vanilla. Seal and massage the contents until well mixed.

Cut 6 12-inch aluminum foil sheets, stacking them on top of each other. Place 1 orange cup on top of stack.

Create a piping bag by pressing the cake batter away from one of the bottom corners of the ziplock bag, and cut the corner off. Pipe the batter into the orange cup, filling to about halfway.

Wrap the orange cup by pulling up the aluminum foil sheet and twisting at the top to tighten. (You should be left with a foil tail at the top, which will help maneuver the cups around the fire.) Set aside trying to keep upright as much as possible. Repeat for each orange cup.

Place the wrapped orange cups around the perimeter of your campfire and rotate every 5 minutes for 10 to 15 minutes. Peek in on one after 10 minutes, poking the batter with a knife to see if it is cooked. If the knife doesn't come out clean, continue cooking for another 5 minutes or so.

Chocolate Pudding Cake

Yield: 4 to 6 servings

Prep Time: 5 minutes

Cook Time: 10 minutes

1 cup all-purpose flour

²/₃ cup sugar

¼ cup cocoa powder

½ teaspoon baking soda

¼ teaspoon kosher salt plus more for serving

²/₃ cup milk

⅓ cup canola oil, plus more for greasing the skillet

1 tablespoon vinegar

1 teaspoon vanilla extract

¼ cup semisweet chocolate chips

OPTIONAL GARNISHES

Heath Bar crumbles

Toasted almond pieces

Whipped cream

TOOLS

Car Camping Base Kit

Medium mixing bowl

Whisk

10-inch cast iron skillet

Heatproof gloves

When my twins, Asha and Ravi, turned four, they wanted a beach camping birthday party. Beach camping in Southern California needs to be booked far in advance, even in their birthday month of October, and I hadn't reserved a campsite, so we were out of luck. Plan B had us heading to our local mountains. It was really cold, and threatening to rain, but we persisted. Then, right when we were about to start the campfire where I planned to make their cake, a ranger stopped by to tell us we couldn't have a fire that day. The whole trip was starting to feel like a fail, but determined to save it, I decided to bake the cake on the stovetop instead, which made the normal classic chocolate cake into more of a moist, steamed cake. I changed the name from Chocolate Cake to Chocolate Pudding Cake—and it was the win we needed. Serve it plain or top it with whipped cream, toffee pieces, or some chopped nuts. —*Aimee*

AT HOME

In a ziplock bag or lidded container, combine the flour, sugar, cocoa powder, baking soda, and salt.

AT CAMP

Make the cake batter: In a medium bowl, whisk together the milk, oil, vinegar, and vanilla. Add the flour mixture and whisk to combine.

In a cast iron skillet, heat about a tablespoon of oil over medium heat. Add the cake batter. Cook for about 1 minute, then stir, scraping the bottom of the skillet with your spatula (just like you're scrambling eggs). Continue to cook for about 5 minutes, stirring and scraping the bottom of the skillet frequently, until the batter thickens and starts to clump together. Remove from the heat, sprinkle the chocolate chips on top, and cover with a lid just long enough for the chocolate chips to melt, about 2 minutes and serve immediately. Optionally, sprinkle with salt, Heath Bar crumbles, almonds, and whipped cream.

Pecan Praline Fondue

Yield: 4 servings

Prep Time: 5 minutes

Cook Time: 30 minutes

¹/₂ cup sugar

1 tablespoon whiskey or water

1¹/₂ tablespoons butter

¹/₂ cup heavy whipping cream

¹/₄ teaspoon kosher salt

¹/₂ cup chopped pecans

FOR SERVING

Sliced green apple

Sliced banana

Marshmallows

Cookies, such as gingersnaps or shortbread

TOOLS

Car Camping Base Kit

Small saucepan

I am not a baker. So when it was decided that I would be the first one to test this recipe while cooking for a beach party in Florida, I laughed out loud and cringed inside. I used a caramel recipe as a guide, which assured me that if the sugar seized up "a bit" during the caramelization process, that's fine. Mine dried out almost completely before browning at all, so I turned off the stove and moved on to the next step of adding milk and butter. It did *not* dissolve the sugar, and looked like a clumpy, liquidy, white mess. I put it back on the stovetop and stirred for what felt like forever, thinking it would end in disaster. Eventually, the mixture evened out in texture and was surprisingly delicious! Being in the South at the time, all I could think of was pralines. When I got back home and shared the recipe with Aimee (who was impressed), she added a sprinkling of pecans on top to finish that thought. This remains one of my proudest moments. —*Emily*

Put the sugar and whiskey in a saucepan and place over medium heat, stirring to combine. Cook until the sugar melts and then clumps up, about 10 to 15 minutes, stirring occasionally. (It can begin to brown, but no need to get it to a dark amber color like other caramels.)

When the sugar has seized up, remove it from heat and slowly stir in the butter, being careful to avoid spatters. Stir in the cream and salt. Return the pan to medium heat and cook until the fondue has slightly thickened. Sprinkle with chopped pecans. Serve with apples, bananas, marshmallows, and cookies.

Maple Syrup Dumplings (Grands-Pères)

Yield: 4 servings

Prep Time: 5 minutes

Cook Time: 15 minutes

½ cup all-purpose flour

1 pinch of kosher salt

1 teaspoon baking powder

1 tablespoon butter, cubed

¼ cup milk

1 cup real maple syrup

FOR SERVING

Whipping cream or whole cream

TOOLS

Car Camping Base Kit

Medium mixing bowl

Medium skillet

Coming from Quebec, I have strong opinions about maple syrup. Canada produces 71 percent of the world's pure maple syrup and of that 91 percent comes from Quebec. So, it's a big deal. These Maple Syrup Dumplings are Daniel's dad's go-to dessert, which he will gladly whip up for anyone who shows the slightest interest. (Jury's still out on whether he's striving to be the ultimate host or just needs an excuse to make some for himself.) —*Mai-Yan*

AT HOME

Prepare the dry ingredients: In a lidded container, combine flour, salt, and baking powder.

AT CAMP

Pour the flour mixture into a medium bowl, and add the butter. Using a fork, mix in the butter until no large chunks are visible. Add the milk and mix until no dry flour remains. (You should have a thick, sticky dough.)

Pour the maple syrup into a medium skillet and bring to a boil over high heat. With a spoon, drop tablespoon-sized blobs of dough into the boiling syrup, being careful not to crowd them as they will expand while cooking. Reduce boil to an active simmer. Let dumplings cook for 5 minutes, then turn and cook for another 2 minutes. Take a sneak peek at the inside of one of the dumplings by gently prying it open on one side with a fork. Dumplings are ready when the dough is no longer sticky and looks like fluffy cake.

Serve with whipped cream or a drizzle of whole cream for the complete experience.

Campfire Bananas with Date Caramel

Yield: 4 servings

Prep Time: 15 minutes

Cook Time: 5 minutes

FOR THE CARAMEL

1 cup packed pitted Medjool dates

1/2 cup brown rice syrup

1/2 cup soy or coconut milk

1/4 teaspoon kosher salt

FOR THE BANANAS

4 bananas

4 tablespoons dark chocolate chips or chopped chocolate

4 tablespoons chopped toasted walnuts

TOOLS

Car Camping Base Kit

As much as I love sweets, I often want something that's not going to make me feel guilty about my choice later. When you're camping, it's tricky to balance the desire to make healthy choices and the fun of eating traditional junky camp foods. Campfire Bananas are a delicious compromise. The date caramel is made at home, but the rest of the dessert is assembled at camp and baked on the campfire. Brown rice syrup helps the date caramel to have that sticky, caramel-like texture, without being overly sweet, so it's worth seeking out even if it's not in your pantry. You can find it at most natural foods stores. —*Aimee*

AT HOME

Make the date caramel: In the bowl of a food processor fitted with the metal blade attachment (or a blender) combine the dates, brown rice syrup, milk, and salt. Blend until it's smooth and looks like caramel. (If your dates are dried out, you may want to soak them in hot water for about an hour before blending.) Store in a jar and keep chilled.

AT CAMP

Cut 4 pieces of aluminum foil large enough to fully wrap around a banana.

Cut a slit lengthwise in each banana, slicing through the peel and the banana but not through the peel on the bottom side. Place each banana on a piece of aluminum foil. Spread the inside of each banana with a tablespoon or two of the date caramel, and then add about a tablespoon each of chocolate and walnuts. Wrap the aluminum foil tightly around each banana.

Place bananas on a grate set over a campfire or directly in the coals, and cook for about 5 minutes or long enough for the banana to soften and the chocolate to melt.

Dirty Gourmet S'moresgasbord

Prep Time: 2 minutes

Cook Time: 1 minute

Graham crackers

Marshmallows

Toppings of your choice
(see Variations)

TOOLS

Roasting stick

We have become sort of famous for our s'mores. Since our blog launch party on New Year's Eve in 2009, we've continually developed new gourmet variations of the traditional s'mores. We even made a "s'moresgasbord" for my wedding in 2014. We continue our quest to find more additions to the gourmet s'mores family, but here are five of our current favorite combinations. —*Emily*

You know how it's done! Sandwich your perfectly roasted marshmallow and toppings between two graham cracker squares. Eat immediately!

Variations:

Strawberry Cheesecake S'more: 1 tablespoon cream cheese, a drizzle of honey, and a couple of strawberry slices.

Birthday Cake S'more: 1 tablespoon vanilla frosting and a couple shakes of rainbow sprinkles.

White Chocolate Lemon S'more: 1 tablespoon lemon curd and a square of white chocolate.

Dark Chocolate, Cookie Butter, and Sea Salt S'more: 1 tablespoon cookie butter, a couple shakes of sea salt, and 1 small square of dark chocolate.

Peanut Butter Maple Bacon S'more: 1 tablespoon peanut butter, 1 teaspoon maple syrup, 1 small square milk chocolate, and ½ strip cooked bacon.

BACKCOUNTRY CAMPING

Car camping and day trips will always be a part of our lives, but the farther into the wilderness we get, the happier we seem to become. These experiences leave deep impressions in our memories and crack open our ideas about possibility. They also give us some bragging rights—and for good reason. We return with stories about mileage, elevation, nights out, and peak-bagging, and with a sense of confidence that is hard to come by another way. This is what we love about backcountry camping. But they don't all have to be epic adventures; they can also be quick resets in the middle of the work week. Either way, food is a key part of your experience out there, so planning is crucial.

BASICS

The recipes in this section fit into many different types of backcountry adventures, defined as being away from most conveniences of the modern human world and likely including all-day physical activity—hiking, cycling, paddling, or umpteen other possibilities. Unlike car camping, where there is access to coolers, cast iron pots, cooking grates, and the like, our backcountry recipes take into account things like weight, space, perishability, and nutritional value as much as possible. Though you will see the occasional "glampacking" recipe, best eaten next to an alpine lake on a low-mileage day, most of these recipes also assume you'll be exhausted by dinnertime, so their methods are simple and quick.

Whether you are backpacking on an alpine trail or bike-packing alongside a scenic river, meals are as much a part of the soul-cleansing experience as bear sightings, shooting stars, sweeping vistas, and glorious mountaintop sunrises. These recipes taste as good as if you made them at home, so they act as a great motivator on that last push up the hill before setting up camp for the night.

BACKCOUNTRY CONSIDERATIONS

The following categories represent some factors that make backcountry recipes unique. Please consider them all before choosing which meals to bring with you.

Weight: Whatever you bring, you have to transport yourself, and it all adds up in weight. Water is one of the most important, but heaviest, items you'll need in the backcountry. Use dehydrated and freeze-dried ingredients to help reduce your overall food weight during travel, but make sure you'll hit a water source by mealtime.

Space/Volume: There's only so much room in your pack, so what you bring better be absolutely necessary! When packing backcountry meals, it's best to remove ingredients from their original packaging. Ideally, you want to portion each meal, bringing only as much as is needed for the recipe. This will save some precious space and also reduce weight in your pack. Our preferred

method is to package meals into ziplock bags (even nesting bags inside one another for particular meals) and write the recipe name along with any at camp instructions (e.g., Add 2 cups of water) with a permanent marker.

Perishability: Without access to a cooler, you have to rely on ingredients that won't spoil in the environment you're traveling in. If you're in a colder environment, you have more options for fresh ingredients than if it's very hot outside. Dry environments offer more options than humid. Dehydrated and freeze-dried ingredients work well in most cases. Throughout these recipes, you'll see our recommendations for fresh ingredients that generally keep better than others. For instance, an avocado and a lime will usually survive—and make you very popular at camp.

Durability: Food isn't the only thing you're packing on your back, in your boat, or on your bike. All of your ingredients will likely be squished in tight next to everything else you are bringing. Everything needs to hold up to be useful.

Nutritional Value: It is difficult to recommend a specific amount of calories needed for a trip because there are a lot of variables involved in making that determination, including:

- How many miles will you be traveling?
- How much elevation gain?
- How warm is the weather?
- What size of a person are you?
- How much weight are you carrying?
- How long is your trip?
- How fast are you traveling?

The other factor involved in nutrition is whether you're actually motivated to eat enough of something to count. A recipe can focus *only* on calorie density, and completely neglect flavor. No matter how hungry you get, you're not likely to eat enough to fully recover from a strenuous day in the backcountry unless it tastes good. Besides, you deserve a satisfying and comforting meal for your efforts! In this section of the book, most recipes will be one-pot meals that include the main components of a balanced, energy-rich meal: carbs, protein, and fat. Each recipe includes a nutritional breakdown estimate to help you plan.

BACKCOUNTRY BASE KIT

The tools you bring on a backcountry trip need to be carefully considered for the same reasons as the ingredients. You don't want to have a bunch of "just in case" tools that will add weight and take up precious space in your pack. Here are two lists. The first is the Backcountry Base Kit, what we consider essentials; the second is our Backcountry Kitchen Niceties, add-ons needed for specific recipes.

- [ ] 1-liter pot with lid
- [ ] Bandana
- [ ] Matches/lighter
- [ ] Pocket knife
- [ ] Salt and pepper
- [ ] Spork
- [ ] Stove with simmer control

BACKCOUNTRY KITCHEN NICETIES

- [ ] ½-liter pot with lid
- [ ] Chef's and/or paring knife with sheath
- [ ] Coffeepot
- [ ] Collapsible backpacking toaster
- [ ] Cutting board
- [ ] Double-walled mug
- [ ] Foldable ladle
- [ ] Foldable spatula
- [ ] LED tea light candles
- [ ] Lightweight plates or bowls
- [ ] Pot scraper
- [ ] Sponge and biodegradable soap

ORGANIZING YOUR BACKCOUNTRY CAMP KITCHEN

When you arrive at camp, the first thing you should do is pick out the best spot for your sleeping area and the best place for your kitchen. These two areas should be a good distance away from one another and also from any natural water sources like streams and lakes. We often get asked if it's OK to cook in the vestibule of a tent. The answer is *no*. Doing so puts you at risk for carbon monoxide poisoning, melting your only shelter, and creating delicious smells that may lure creatures directly into your bed.

Choose a kitchen area that is in a relatively flat location, and (ideally) sheltered from wind and weather. We usually cook on the ground, but if you're lucky enough to find a nice flat rock, use it! Keep all of your food activities in this kitchen area for the duration of your stay.

MEAL PLANNING

We keep emphasizing how important it is to devote time to proper meal planning *before* your trip. Things will invariably come up, so planning helps you be as prepared as possible. Mai-Yan writes out her entire menu in a tiny journal she brings with her on every trip. Emily prefers an index card or sticky note thrown into her bear canister for easy recall during mealtime. Either way, it's a good idea to think through when you expect to eat what. You can always make adjustments if necessary, but it's nice to not *have* to make this decision unless you choose to.

THE DIRTY GOURMET BACKCOUNTRY RECIPE FORMULA

We think of our backcountry recipes first as basic formulas. Here is a breakdown of how to build a meal.

Grains, Noodles, or Potatoes: This is the base of your meal. Carbs from grains, noodles, or potatoes fill you up and give you the energy to get going in the morning. You want to choose things that don't need too much water and that have a short cook time. Couscous, egg noodles, angel hair pasta, instant mashed potatoes, or parboiled rice are good choices.

Veggies and Protein: Vegetables and protein are critical for keeping your meal substantial and balanced. Protein is important for much-needed recovery, and fiber will keep things moving along. We like to use fresh vegetables like carrots and broccoli, and sturdy greens like kale. When it's getting late in the trip, you'll likely have to use dehydrated or freeze-dried veggies—there are a lot of options but mushrooms, peas, and corn are good, reliable standbys. As for protein, experiment with canned chicken and tuna, bean flakes, smoked fish, and nuts and seeds.

Spices and Seasoning: This is what is going to give your dish its personality and taste. The most common seasonings used are salt, pepper, and packable dried bouillon. For something more exciting, experiment with spices you have at home, but pre-measure them before your trip so you don't have to carry a whole spice pantry with you.

Texture: Backpacking recipes tend to be mushy by nature, so we always recommend topping your meal with some crunch. Try leftover snacks like chips, crackers, nuts—or our Savory Granola (see On the Trail, Savory Snacks).

BACKCOUNTRY INGREDIENTS

There are a lot of ingredients easily found at your neighborhood supermarket, but keep your eyes peeled at specialty grocers, such as international, farmers', or vegetarian markets. You can also get a lot of useful ingredients online and sometimes at your local outdoor gear shop to add flavor to your backpacking meals.

In your hunt for backcountry meals, you will likely come across various freeze-dried and dehydrated ingredients. These are two distinct methods, created using different processes and are different in nature as a result. Freeze-dried ingredients are usually crispier and they

MEAL PLANNING HOW-TO

Here's how we do it:

- **Write down a list of all meals that you need to plan for.** For instance, a three-day backpacking trip will usually require lunch and dinner the first day; breakfast, lunch, and dinner the second day; and simply breakfast for the third.

- **Fill in an idea for each.** This can even be something you like to eat at home that you plan to adjust for backpacking later.

- **Go through each idea or recipe** and figure out how to make it backcountry friendly. (Don't worry, this chapter should provide a lot of inspiration!)

- **Consider the specifics of the day when selecting recipes.** If you're planning on doing a lot of mileage one day, make sure you're setting yourself up for a quick, easy, and filling dinner. If you'd like to try a more complicated recipe, plan to make it on a day when you don't have as much going on or are staying put for the day. If you want to bring some fresh ingredients, expect to use them early on in the trip.

- **Pack your written menu in an easy-to-find-at-mealtime spot.** Make immediate notes for any changes or variations you come up with for your next trip. These meal plan lists are more than a set of notes, they are also fun souvenirs to remind you of your great adventures.

rehydrate faster. Dehydrated ingredients tend to be less expensive and can be homemade more easily.

Dehydrated vegetables are great for getting texture and nutrition in backcountry meals, but some—such as peas, carrots, and onion flakes—need a longer soak time than others to rehydrate. Pre-soaking dehydrated vegetables (while setting up camp) helps soften them without adding cook time and using up precious fuel reserves.

Here's a list of some of our favorite multiuse ingredients. You can be ready for a trip at any moment with these items on hand.

- Bouillon cubes
- Coconut milk powder
- Coconut oil
- Dehydrated bean flakes
- Freeze-dried peas
- Instant miso soup
- Maple sugar

- Peanut butter powder/nut butter packets
- Powdered eggs
- Smoked salmon
- Soba noodles, angel hair nests, ramen, rice noodles
- Tomato powder
- Instant mashed potatoes

DEHYDRATING YOUR OWN FOOD

We have often dehydrated food in the oven, which is very easy. A dehydrator is a worthy specialty item, but it's not a requirement for making your own backpacking meals or using our recipes. If you're interested in doing more of your own dehydration, however, you won't regret the investment. You'll be impressed with the versatility a dehydrator gives you, from creating unique sauces to utilizing delicate ingredients like eggs more frequently. Homemade dehydrated food tends to rehydrate better and taste fresher than store-bought versions. Check out our website for dehydrator recipes if you're interested.

COOKING IN THE BACKCOUNTRY

If you're lucky enough to find a backcountry location that allows campfires, you can refer to the Appendix and make aluminum foil pouch meals. If you will be dependent on a stove, you can choose to either cook directly in your pot, or rehydrate your meal in a reusable heatproof bag. We have a long-standing debate on which is better.

Aimee: There is no reason to bring a reusable bag for cooking. A pot can do it all.

Emily: I've had a few traumatizing experiences where my coffee tasted reminiscent of the beef stew I made the night before. I'd rather have one small pot and a collapsible bag than a large pot and potentially a small one as well.

Aimee: Just clean your pot! Anyway, it's easier to clean a pot than a bag, with all its nooks and crannies.

Emily: I keep my pot clean to make water for cooking, drinking, and cleaning. I cannot fit a dirty pot into my bear canister if I don't clean it perfectly, which is sometimes impossible outdoors. I prefer to keep all the food tastes and smells quarantined to a single vessel.

Aimee: My food stays hotter because I cook it to completion rather than having to wait up to 20 minutes for rehydration.

Emily: I save fuel by simply using it to boil water, and letting my insulated bag do the rest of the work. A bonus is that I can hold my warm food bag near my belly to keep me warm while I wait. You could rehydrate in a pot, but you'd need to figure out a way to insulate it.

The conversation continues, and there will always be debates like this in the world of backcountry cooking. It is nice for us to have so many different perspectives in one small group so we are exposed to the benefits of each style. We debate about using a pot versus a bag, about what types of pots, and about what types of stoves. For the purpose of this cookbook, we came to an agreement about the best type of stove to recommend to make virtually all of our backcountry recipes—a stove with good simmer control. We rest our opinions there.

CRITTER PROOFING AND CLEANUP

Just as limiting your kitchen gear to one section of camp is important, the cleanup you perform before walking away from that space is essential to preserving the safety of your group and all future visitors to that location—both humans and wildlife. Visiting the wild places of the world comes with a responsibility to keep those places equally as wild when you leave. If you cook, you need to clean and keep the impact on the local flora and fauna minimal, if not nonexistent.

Every area has its own regulations for dealing with food properly. In California, where we live, most backcountry areas require you to carry a bear-proof canister. Some locations allow for bags of food to be hung in trees, but this takes practice and needs to be done properly to be truly effective. When we went backpacking in grizzly country in Canada, there were thirty-foot bear poles installed and food was hung with ease. The purpose of bear-proofing is definitely to keep you safe from large wildlife, but it also protects your food from smaller forest creatures.

Food waste should be packed out with you under all circumstances. Though fruit peelings and coffee grounds are biodegradable and natural, they are generally not natural to the area you're in. Here are some tips to make cleanup fast and effective.

- Bring biodegradable soap and a scrubby for easy cleanup. Make sure to establish your cleanup area at least 200 feet from natural water sources in the area. It is not OK to dump food or clean dishes directly in natural water sources.

- Use hot water to help remove stuck-on bits of food. It turns the leftovers in your pot into a nice soup. If you can get someone in your group to drink that, you'll have nothing to pack out.
- Provide something delicious like a piece of bread or a tortilla to sop up the last bits of food in a pot if you're not into the idea of drinking leftover "soup."
- Use snow, leaves, or even pine needles as a natural abrasive.
- Pack out any leftovers you can't consume. If there's a little bit of food-flavored water left in the pot, it's OK to scatter it far from camp.

RECIPES

BREAKFASTS

DINNERS

DRINKS

DESSERTS

BREAKFASTS

Cheddar Bacon Pancakes

Yield: 6 (5-inch) pancakes
Prep Time: 5 minutes
Cook Time: 15 minutes

½ cup all-purpose flour

¼ cup plus 1 tablespoon cheddar cheese powder

¼ cup milk powder

¼ cup bacon crumbles

2 tablespoons freeze-dried chives

1 tablespoon dehydrated eggs

2 teaspoons baking powder

½ teaspoon kosher salt

1¼ cups water

2 tablespoons vegetable oil, divided

4 tablespoons maple syrup

TOOLS

Backcountry Base Kit
Long-handled spoon
Nonstick backpacking skillet
Spatula

This is one of our most popular car camping recipes and is our signature breakfast when we cater outdoor events. While many are initially taken aback by our bastardization of the universally loved pancake, they soon realize Cheddar Bacon Pancakes are "legit." Here's our backcountry version where you'll always get first dibs. —*Mai-Yan*

AT HOME

Prepare the dry ingredients: In a gallon-size ziplock bag, combine the flour, cheese powder, milk powder, bacon crumbles, freeze-dried chives, dehydrated eggs, baking powder, and salt.

AT CAMP

Add the water to the ziplock bag of dry ingredients. Seal and massage the bag to combine, until no dry flour remains. Open the bag and set on a level surface. Roll down the edges to make it easier to spoon out the batter.

Heat about a teaspoon of oil in a skillet over medium-low heat. Add enough batter to the skillet to form a 5-inch diameter pancake. Cook until bubbles form, about 2 to 3 minutes. Flip the pancake and cook until the pancake is cooked through, about another 1 to 2 minutes. Repeat with the remaining batter.

Serve the pancakes hot with maple syrup.

Serving Size: ½ of recipe; Calories: 570; Protein: 19 g; Fat: 28 g; Saturated Fat: 10 g; Carbohydrates: 58 g; Fiber: 1 g; Sugar: 29 g

CHEDDAR BACON PANCAKES (PG 189)

BREAKFAST COUSCOUS WITH DATES AND TAHINI

Breakfast Couscous with Dates and Tahini

Yield: 2 servings

Prep Time: 10 minutes

Cook Time: 10 minutes

1/4 cup milk powder

1/8 teaspoon nutmeg

1 1/2 cups water

2/3 cup couscous

6 medjool dates, pitted and chopped

4 tablespoons tahini

TOOLS

Backcountry Base Kit

For my thirtieth birthday, I decided to celebrate by going on a three-day backpacking trip in the Golden Trout Wilderness. This trip is now known as the *Golden Trout Fiasco*. As we finished packing up at the trailhead, we did a quick inventory of the food and discovered we had four sweaty bricks of cheese among the three of us—it was only 8:00 AM and it was already 80 degrees. After ditching some cheese, we decided to book it to gain some elevation and escape the increasing temperatures.

The anticipation of a new adventure quickly turned into horror as beautiful meadows revealed themselves as festering grounds for thousands of hungry mosquitos. The heat remained with us and more than a few meals went bad leaving slimy messes we had to carry out with us. One of the true all-weather backcountry meals that did hold up was a variation on this Breakfast Couscous recipe. It was the morale and energy boost we needed to conquer the nearby eleven-thousand-foot peak where we got a brief respite from mosquitos and an amazing vista on the Kern River.

Lessons learned: (1) Plan meals appropriately for the weather, (2) Adventure with people who will still love you after seeing you at your worst, and (3) count on Breakfast Couscous to see you through. —*Mai-Yan*

AT HOME

Combine the milk powder and nutmeg in a small ziplock bag.

AT CAMP

In a 1-liter pot, bring the water to a boil over high heat. Add the milk powder and nutmeg, stirring until no lumps remain. Remove from heat and stir in the couscous. Cover and let sit for about 5 minutes.

To serve, divide the couscous into two portions and top each with chopped dates and tahini.

Serving Size: 1/2 the recipe; Calories: 700; Protein: 18 g; Fat: 23 g; Saturated Fat: 5 g; Carbohydrates: 107 g; Fiber: 9 g; Sugar: 53 g

Hungry Camper Creamy Oats

Yield: 2 servings

Prep Time: 5 minutes

Cook Time: 10 minutes

1 cup rolled oats

½ cup dried bing cherries, roughly chopped

⅓ cup whole milk powder

¼ cup raisins

1 tablespoon brown sugar

½ teaspoon kosher salt

2 tablespoons shredded coconut

2 tablespoons toasted hazelnuts, crushed

2 cups water

TOOLS

Backcountry Base Kit

Big Sur is one of the famous destinations along the Pacific Coast Highway. Tall, sheer cliffs overlooking the ocean, side by side with a thousand acres of Pfeiffer Big Sur State Park makes for an impressive sight that is totally worth the hype. This was our playground for Aimee's birthday backpacking trip. We designed it as a leisurely backpacking trip, not striving for big miles every day but instead fully enjoying time at camp—made even better when we found a furnished campsite with DIY stone benches, a fire ring, and a vista of the ocean in the distance. In the spirit of leisureliness, we kept the meals simple and made ourselves good old oatmeal for breakfast, which is the perfect blank canvas for your yummy fixings. We threw everything we had in the pantry into this recipe to create a loaded breakfast that has as many toppings as it has oats. —*Mai-Yan*

We prefer rolled oats over instant oatmeal since it has more texture and flavor. One way to quicken cook time is to add the oats to the water before it even boils. This will also act as a presoak, making for a creamier result.

AT HOME

In a large ziplock bag, combine the oats, cherries, milk powder, raisins, brown sugar, and salt.

In a small ziplock bag, combine the coconut and hazelnuts and tuck it inside the bag with the oat mixture.

AT CAMP

In a 1-liter pot, bring the water to a boil over high heat, then immediately add the oat mix.

Return to a boil and reduce to a simmer. Cover for 10 minutes and continue cooking on low, stirring often. Remove from heat.

To serve, divide the oatmeal into two portions and sprinkle with coconut and hazelnuts.

Serving Size: ½ the recipe; Calories: 760; Protein: 18 g; Fat: 34 g; Saturated Fat: 6 g; Carbohydrates: 100 g; Fiber: 11 g; Sugar: 30 g

Fried Grits Scramble with Greens, Leeks, and Bacon

Yield: 2 servings

Prep Time: 10 minutes

Cook Time: 2 to 3 hours at home, 10 minutes at camp

1 cup chopped fresh greens, such as collards

1 leek, sliced

2 cups water

2 packets instant grits

1 tablespoon coconut oil

⅓ cup grated Parmesan cheese

1 tablespoon bacon bits

<u>TOOLS</u>

Backcountry Base Kit

Nonstick backpacking skillet, any size

Aimee and I both have a lot of family in North Carolina. It's where all our parents came from, and where all our extended family still is. We are West Coasters, but we know about grits. I consider myself a grits connoisseur, sourcing them from all sorts of small local places around the state of North Carolina. The only kind of grits I can find in California are instant grits, which are barely acceptable in my home, but are perfect for backpacking. This recipe is a fancied-up grits dish with flavor that is reminiscent of shrimp and grits, which is a delicacy in *South* Carolina, but I'll take it. —*Emily*

AT HOME

Preheat the oven to its lowest setting, about 170°F.

Arrange greens and leeks in a single layer on a rimmed baking sheet, and place in oven for 2 to 3 hours, until dry. Let cool, then store in a ziplock bag.

AT CAMP

In a 1-liter pot, bring the water to a boil over high heat. Pour off about ⅓ cup water into each packet of grits and let rehydrate directly in the packages. (Alternatively, you can rehydrate the grits in a mug or bowl.)

Add the dried vegetables to the pot of water, cover, and let rehydrate for about 5 minutes.

Heat the oil in a skillet on medium high heat. Add the grits and scramble until the mixture just starts to brown, about 5 minutes.

Drain the vegetables and add them to the grits. Sprinkle with Parmesan and toss to combine. Remove from heat.

To serve, divide the grits into two portions and sprinkle with bacon bits.

Serving Size: ½ the recipe; Calories: 320; Protein: 14 g; Fat: 15 g; Saturated Fat: 10 g; Carbohydrates: 32 g; Fiber: 3 g; Sugar: 2 g

HUNGRY CAMPER CREAMY OATS (PG 192)

FRIED GRITS SCRAMBLE WITH GREENS, LEEKS, AND BACON (PG 193)

SUMMER SAUSAGE PESTO OMELET (PG 196)

QUINOA CRUNCH PANCAKES (PG 197)

Summer Sausage Pesto Omelet

Yield: 2 servings

Prep Time: 5 minutes

Cook Time: 10 minutes

4 tablespoons powdered eggs

4 teaspoons creamy pesto powdered sauce mix

¼ teaspoon kosher salt

½ cup water

1 tablespoon vegetable oil

⅓ cup summer sausage, diced

TOOLS

Backcountry Base Kit

Nonstick skillet

Spatula

There's something official about starting the day with eggs, which makes this recipe, breakfast with a capital "B." We have no qualms about using powdered eggs since they really do rehydrate exactly like fresh eggs. Summer sausage is one of the few meat items that is OK to bring in the backcountry since it is cured and doesn't require refrigeration. It's good as a snack and can supplement meals like this omelet. If you want to treat yourself, pack some tortillas or a bagel to have with your Breakfast. —*Mai-Yan*

AT HOME

Combine the powdered eggs, pesto sauce mix, and salt in a large ziplock bag.

AT CAMP

Add the water to the egg-pesto bag, seal, and massage contents to mix well.

Heat the oil in a skillet over high heat. When it is hot, add the egg mixture. Lower the flame to medium. You will notice the edges cooking first. As they do, swirl more and more of the egg mixture to the edges to cook all of it. Continue until the omelet has almost no runny eggs left in it. (You may need to lower your flame so the underside of the omelet doesn't burn.)

Add the sausage. With a spatula, start pulling away the edges of the omelet from the skillet edge until you can eventually slip your spatula underneath. Fold omelet in half and remove from heat.

Serving Size: ½ of recipe; Calories: 250; Protein: 9 g; Fat: 18 g; Saturated Fat: 4 g; Carbohydrates: 13 g; Fiber: 1 g; Sugar: 1 g

Quinoa Crunch Pancakes

Yield: 6 (5-inch) pancakes
Prep Time: 5 minutes
Cook Time: 15 minutes

¼ cup quinoa
½ cup all-purpose flour
¼ cup rolled oats
¼ cup milk powder
1 tablespoon ground flaxseed
1 tablespoon brown sugar
1 teaspoon baking powder
½ teaspoon baking soda
Pinch of kosher salt
3 tablespoons maple sugar
1 cup plus 2 tablespoons water
1 tablespoon vegetable oil, plus
more for your skillet

TOOLS

Backcountry Base Kit
Nonstick backpacking skillet
Spatula

Pancakes in the backcountry are a treat, and they aren't that difficult to make. The problem I come across is that they don't really sustain me for very long. Inspired to make a heartier pancake, I experimented with using quinoa and oats to really bulk them up with a boost of protein and fiber. The quinoa is mixed into the batter raw, so it adds a subtle crunch that I love. —*Aimee*

AT HOME

In a dry skillet over medium heat, toast the quinoa, shaking the skillet often. Once it's brown and smells toasty, remove from the heat and set aside to cool slightly.

In a food processor or blender, combine toasted quinoa, flour, oats, milk powder, flaxseed, brown sugar, baking powder, baking soda, and salt. Process on high speed until the quinoa is broken up a bit and the ingredients are thoroughly combined, about 1 minute. Transfer the mixture to a quart-size ziplock bag.

Put the maple sugar in a small ziplock bag, and tuck it into the larger bag.

AT CAMP

Add 1 cup of water and 1 tablespoon oil to the flour mixture in the ziplock bag. Massage the bag to combine, until no dry flour remains.

In a skillet over medium heat, heat a teaspoon of oil. Pour about ¼ cup of batter into the skillet and cook until small bubbles form, about 2 to 3 minutes. Flip the pancake and cook until cooked through, about another 1 to 2 minutes. Repeat with the remaining batter.

While the pancakes are cooking, make the maple syrup. Add 2 tablespoons of water to the ziplock bag of the maple sugar. Seal and squish the bag to combine.

Serve the pancakes hot with maple syrup.

Serving Size: ½ of recipe; Calories: 460; Protein: 12 g; Fat: 15 g; Saturated Fat: 4 g; Carbohydrates: 69 g; Fiber: 4 g; Sugar: 24 g

Breakfast Burritos

Yield: 4 burritos

Prep Time: 15 minutes

Cook Time: 15 minutes

¾ cup dehydrated eggs (equivalent to 6 eggs)

1 teaspoon taco seasoning

¼ teaspoon kosher salt

¼ teaspoon freshly ground black pepper

1½ cups water for hash browns

1 (4.2-ounce) box of dehydrated hash browns

1 cup plus 2 tablespoons water for egg mixture

4 (8-inch) soft flour tortillas

1 avocado, halved and pit removed

1 lime, quartered

1 tablespoon extra-virgin olive oil

¾ cup grated cheddar cheese

Kosher salt and freshly ground black pepper, to taste

Hot sauce of choice

TOOLS

Backcountry Base Kit

Nonstick backpacking skillet

Spatula or spoon

My husband told me one day: "Whenever a burrito is a menu item, don't let me order anything else." The thing is, he manages to turn whatever he is eating into a burrito, wrapping just about anything into the confines of a tortilla. I lovingly refer to these creations as "shit burritos." Needless to say, burritos are important to our family. The burrito form is an excellent way to transport food, which is nice if you like to get on the trail before you're ready to eat. These Breakfast Burritos are the kind of burritos that we fantasize about eating *after* a trip is over, but this recipe is totally doable far from your favorite restaurant! Crispy hash browns and smooth avocado round out this delicious breakfast. —*Emily*

AT HOME

Combine the dehydrated eggs, taco seasoning, salt, and pepper in a gallon-size ziplock bag.

AT CAMP

In a small saucepan, bring 1½ cups of water to a boil over high heat, then pour it into the dehydrated hash brown carton. Close and set aside for a minimum of 12 minutes.

To the egg mixture in the ziplock bag, add 1 cup plus 2 tablespoons of water and seal. Massage contents until well mixed.

Across the center of each tortilla, smash a quarter of the avocado, followed by a squeeze of lime juice. Set aside.

Heat the oil in a skillet over medium heat. Add the hash browns and fry until they are golden brown, about 5 minutes. Transfer from the skillet and divide hash browns between the four tortillas.

Pour the egg mixture into the skillet and scramble until cooked through, about 5 minutes, then remove from heat. Add the cheese to eggs and stir so the cheese melts. Add salt and pepper to taste. Divide the egg mixture evenly across the four tortillas.

Use your best burrito wrapping skills to get each tortilla closed up. If you don't plan to eat these burritos immediately, wrap them tightly in foil and see how long you can resist.

When serving, don't forget the hot sauce!

Serving Size: 1 burrito; Calories: 480; Protein: 18 g; Fat: 31 g; Saturated Fat: 10 g; Carbohydrates: 30 g; Fiber: 5 g; Sugar: 1 g

English Muffin French Toast with Peach Syrup

Yield: 2 servings

Prep Time: 5 minutes

Cook Time: 15 to 20 minutes

FOR THE FRENCH TOAST

3 tablespoons dried egg powder

1 tablespoon milk powder

½ teaspoon cinnamon

½ cup water

1 tablespoon coconut oil

2 English muffins, cut in half

FOR THE SYRUP

¼ cup maple sugar

⅓ cup chopped dried peaches

¼ cup water

TOOLS

Backcountry Base Kit

Nonstick backpacking skillet

Spatula

The first time I tried using dehydrated eggs was on a trip to a secret spot we named "Earth Baby Lake." We'd hiked over Taboose Pass in the Sierra the day before to find this off-trail lake. It was a difficult journey and we worked up an appetite. I had successfully dehydrated eggs in my new dehydrator, and they powdered beautifully, but I miscalculated how much water was needed to *rehydrate* them, making the French toast quite chewy. The next attempt at French toast was in Banff National Park in Canada made from a fresh loaf of local bread near the trailhead and the cutest tin of Canadian syrup. This worked out pretty well, except we had to be careful not to squish the bread or allow the syrup to leak. We've since landed on English muffins and maple sugar as our ideal combination to solve these dilemmas. English muffins are tougher than many other bread types so they can handle the pack, while maple sugar dissolves perfectly into water to create a leakproof syrup substitute. The process even allows it to absorb other flavors nicely, so we added dried peaches for that much more flavor. —*Emily*

AT HOME

Prepare the dry ingredients: In a large ziplock bag, combine the egg powder, milk powder, and cinnamon. In a second ziplock bag, combine the maple sugar and dried peaches. Tuck this bag inside the larger bag.

AT CAMP

To make the maple syrup, add water to the ziplock bag containing the maple sugar and peaches. Stir well and set aside while you make the French toast. Alternatively, you can heat the sugar mixture in a small pot.

To make the French toast, add the water to the egg mixture in the large ziplock bag. Seal the bag and massage the egg mixture together with your hands until the egg is fully hydrated.

In a skillet over medium heat, heat about half a tablespoon of the coconut oil. Dip one half of an English muffin into the egg mixture,

and set onto the skillet for about 2 minutes. Flip and cook until the egg is cooked through, about another 2 minutes. Wrap the French toast slice in aluminum foil and set aside. Continue cooking the rest of the French toast, adding more coconut oil as needed.

Serve with maple syrup and fruit.

Serving Size: ½ of recipe; Calories: 440; Protein: 10 g; Fat: 13 g; Saturated Fat: 8 g; Carbohydrates: 73 g; Fiber: 7 g; Sugar: 14 g

DINNERS

Black Bean Tortilla Soup

Yield: 2 servings
Prep Time: 10 minutes
Cook Time: About 5 minutes

1 cup dehydrated black bean flakes

½ cup freeze-dried corn

1½ teaspoons tomato powder

1 teaspoon dried onion flakes

1 small bouillon cube (about 1 teaspoon)

½ teaspoon ground cumin

½ teaspoon chili powder

2 cups water

FOR SERVING

½ lime, cut into wedges

½ avocado, cubed

Crushed tortilla chips

TOOLS

Backcountry Base Kit

Cutting board (optional)

We've made this recipe so many times, we could do it blindfolded at this point. We tend to make it at live-cooking demos and workshops because it showcases so well how delicious—and easy—backpacking meals can be when you make them yourself. Bean flakes are a secret weapon of ours for backpacking: they are quick to cook, make everything heartier, and can even be made into refried beans. This soup is great for a crowd. It can be easily customized to suit any dietary needs and is easy to scale to any number of hungry eaters. It should be a standard on every backpacking trip, even just as a backup meal (in case you don't actually catch all those fish). —*Emily*

AT HOME

Into a quart-size ziplock bag, measure out bean flakes, corn, tomato powder, onion flakes, bouillon cube, cumin, and chili powder.

AT CAMP

Add the water into a medium pan, then pour in the black bean mixture and let sit for about 10 minutes or until the onion flakes and corn rehydrate. Over high heat, bring the mixture to a boil and simmer for about 5 minutes, or until the corn is softened.

Serve with a squeeze of lime juice, avocado, and crushed tortilla chips.

Serving Size: ½ of recipe; Calories: 460; Protein: 15 g; Fat: 15 g; Saturated Fat: 2 g; Carbohydrates: 67 g; Fiber: 31 g; Sugar: 7 g

Moroccan Stew with Couscous

Yield: 2 servings

Prep Time: 5 minutes at home, 5 minutes at camp

Cook Time: About 20 minutes

1 tablespoon tomato powder

1 teaspoon kosher salt

1/2 teaspoon cumin

1/2 teaspoon smoked paprika

1/2 teaspoon ground ginger

1/4 teaspoon turmeric

1/4 teaspoon freshly ground black pepper

1/8 teaspoon saffron

1 small red onion

1 medium (about 6 ounces) sweet potato

1 medium (about 6 ounces) potato

1/4 cup pitted olives

2 1/2 cups water, divided

1 cup couscous

1 tablespoon coconut oil

1/4 cup raisins

Juice of 1 lemon, for serving

TOOLS

Backcountry Base Kit

Extra pot, 1 liter or larger

Cutting board (optional)

Last winter, I worked until 2:00 PM on a rare snowy Monday, got to Mount Baldy by 3:00 PM, and had camp set up by 5:00 PM. We got up early the next morning to practice our ice axe self-arresting skills in the Baldy Bowl, and I was back at work by noon. It sounds like an effort, but it truly was rejuvenating and important for my overall health. Energy breeds more energy. And those earned bragging points we mentioned earlier aren't too bad when you get back to work and ask your friends and coworkers what *they* did last night.

This stew is ideal for a speedy trip. Pre-measure the spice mix into a ziplock bag and either chop up your vegetables nice and small at home, or do it at camp. We recommend root vegetables since they last longer than other fresh vegetables. —*Emily*

AT HOME

Measure the tomato powder, salt, cumin, paprika, ginger, turmeric, pepper, and saffron into a small ziplock bag.

AT CAMP

Dice the onion. Dice the sweet potato and potato, leaving the skins on. Set aside. Cut the olives in half, and set aside.

Bring 1 1/2 cups of the water to a boil in a small pot over high heat. Remove from heat, add couscous, cover, and set aside while you cook the stew.

In a large pot, heat the coconut oil over medium-high heat. Add the onions, sweet potato, and potato. Sauté until the onions soften, about 5 minutes. Add the spice mixture and cook for 1 minute. Add the remaining cup of water, raisins, and olives and stir to combine. Reduce the heat to low, cover, and simmer until the vegetables are tender.

Serve over couscous with a squeeze of lemon.

Serving Size: 1/2 the recipe; Calories: 680; Protein: 15 g; Fat: 12 g; Saturated Fat: 7 g; Carbohydrates: 126 g; Fiber: 11 g; Sugar: 19 g

Backcountry Skillet Enchiladas

Yield: 4 enchiladas
Prep Time: 5 minutes
Cook Time: 10 minutes

3 tablespoons tomato powder

2 tablespoons taco seasoning

1/4 teaspoon cayenne pepper

1/4 teaspoon sugar

1 1/2 cups water

1 tablespoon oil

4 (6-inch) soft flour tortillas

1 cup shredded cheddar cheese

8 ounces pre-cooked chicken in a foil pouch or can

FOR SERVING (OPTIONAL)

Shredded cheese garnish

Sliced jalapeños

TOOLS

Backcountry Base Kit

Nonstick backpacking skillet

Spatula

Sometimes—a lot of times, actually—I forget to eat, and by the time I'm starving, nothing sounds good. This makes me cranky and whiny at home, but it can be downright dangerous in the backcountry. It's a big reason why I dedicated a chunk of my life to outdoor cooking. One fix for this issue is creating a set menu that I can look forward to. Another is bringing items I really love to think about while I hike, like enchiladas. There aren't many foods that I eat a full serving of, but I can wolf down a plate of enchiladas in record time. So if enchiladas are part of my backpacking menu, I am set. Homemade enchilada sauce is delicious and easy to make with dried ingredients, and tortillas are an easy item to throw in a bear canister. —*Emily*

AT HOME

Combine the tomato powder, taco seasoning, cayenne, and sugar in a small ziplock bag.

AT CAMP

In a cold skillet, create the enchilada sauce. Add the spice mix, water, and oil, and mix to combine. Set aside.

Sprinkle about 1/4 cup shredded cheese down the middle of each tortilla. Reserve a little cheese for garnish. Next, divide the chicken equally across the 4 tortillas. Tightly roll up each tortilla and place 2 of them in the sauce-filled skillet. (If you happen to have a larger skillet and can fit more, go for it.) Gently roll the tortillas a full rotation in the sauce, ending with the seam side down. You want to coat the tortilla and allow sauce to sneak into the enchilada. Turn the heat on as low as it will go without the flame going out. Simmer for about 2 minutes before gently rotating enchiladas 180 degrees to prevent the tortillas from sticking. Simmer another 3 minutes until cheese inside the enchiladas has melted. Garnish with more cheese and jalapeños as desired. Feel free to eat these right out of the skillet, or transfer to a plate with a drizzle of extra sauce before making the second pair of enchiladas.

Serving Size: 1/2 the recipe; Calories: 600; Protein: 21 g; Fat: 34 g; Saturated Fat: 16 g; Carbohydrates: 52 g; Fiber: 4 g; Sugar: 1 g

Red Lentil Dal

Yield: 2 servings

Prep Time: 5 minutes at home, 5 minutes at camp

Cook Time: 30 to 35 minutes

1 tablespoon tomato powder

³/₄ teaspoon kosher salt

¹/₄ teaspoon coriander

¹/₄ teaspoon cumin

¹/₄ teaspoon cayenne pepper (optional)

¹/₄ teaspoon turmeric

1 small onion, finely chopped

1 tablespoon canola oil

2 cloves garlic, minced

1-inch piece ginger, minced

3 cups water

1 cup red lentils

FOR SERVING

Flatbread or rice

Preserved lemon or Indian pickles

TOOLS

Backcountry Base Kit

Cutting board (optional)

Even though I didn't grow up eating dal, it has become my comfort food. We make it all the time in our family, and it's the one type of "real" food that Asha will always eat happily. This is a very practical backcountry meal since red lentils are easy to find and cook relatively quickly compared to other types of lentils. Also, the spices are warming on a cool night, and the lentils are full of protein and fiber to replenish you after a long day. —*Aimee*

AT HOME

Combine the tomato powder, salt, coriander, cumin, cayenne, and turmeric in a small ziplock bag.

AT CAMP

Combine the onion and oil in a 1-liter pot over medium heat. Sauté the onion until it's softened and slightly caramelized, about 5 to 8 minutes, depending on your stove. Add the garlic and ginger and cook for another 2 minutes. Add the ziplock bag of dry ingredients and stir to combine. Add the water and lentils, increase heat to high, and bring mixture to a boil. Reduce the heat to low and simmer for 20 to 30 minutes, or until lentils are tender.

Serve hot with flatbread or rice and preserved lemon or Indian pickles.

Serving Size: ¹/₂ the recipe (without rice or flatbread); Calories: 340; Protein: 19 g; Fat: 7 g; Saturated Fat: 1 g; Carbohydrates: 47 g; Fiber: 23 g; Sugar: 0 g

Gnocchi with Creamy Sun-Dried Tomato Sauce

Yield: 2 servings

Prep Time: 5 minutes

Cook Time: 5 minutes

¼ cup sun-dried tomatoes (not packed in oil), finely chopped

2 tablespoons tomato powder

½ teaspoon garlic powder

¼ teaspoon sugar

¼ teaspoon kosher salt

¼ teaspoon freshly ground black pepper

1-ounce packet cashew butter

1 pound gnocchi

2 cups water

FOR SERVING (OPTIONAL)

Parmesan cheese

Red pepper flakes

TOOLS

Backcountry Base Kit

Spatula or spoon

Bowl or second pot

I was one of those vegetarians who for years wouldn't go vegan because I couldn't imagine a life without creamy, cheesy things. Luckily my husband, Kismat, got a head start, taking the plunge a few years before I did. Rather than make separate food for him and the rest of us, I learned to cook in a whole new way, where I slowly became convinced that I could give up dairy too. I learned new tricks to satisfy my cravings for rich, creamy foods. It turns out that some of these tricks apply to backcountry cooking, even if you aren't vegan. One of them is to use cashews in place of easily perishable cream. Little pouches of cashew butter are easily found at natural foods stores or online. —Aimee

AT HOME

Combine the sun-dried tomatoes, tomato powder, garlic powder, sugar, salt, and pepper in a large ziplock bag. Place the unopened cashew butter packet in the bag as well.

AT CAMP

Fill a pot with water and bring to a boil over high heat. Carefully drop in the gnocchi. Cook for 3 to 4 minutes, or until cooked through. Turn off the stove and transfer the gnocchi to another container, reserving about 1 cup of the cooking water in the pot. Add the tomato mixture and the cashew butter to the reserved hot water, and mix well to get the sauce as smooth as possible.

Turn the stove back on and heat the sauce, stirring constantly until no tomato powder or cashew butter lumps remain. (Thin with additional water if the sauce seems too thick.) Remove the pot from heat and stir in the gnocchi.

Serve with Parmesan cheese and red pepper flakes if desired.

Serving Size: ½ the recipe; Calories: 830; Protein: 27 g; Fat: 9 g; Saturated Fat: 2 g; Carbohydrates: 167 g; Fiber: 15 g; Sugar: 6 g

RED LENTIL DAL (PG 208)

GNOCCHI WITH CREAMY SUN-DRIED TOMATO SAUCE (PG 209)

LENTIL VEGETABLE STEW WITH DUMPLINGS (PG 212)

SMOKED SALMON AND GRAVY MASHED POTATOES (PG 213)

Lentil Vegetable Stew with Dumplings

Yield: 2 servings

Prep Time: 5 minutes

Cook Time: 15 to 20 minutes

FOR THE STEW

1 cup dehydrated lentils

3 tablespoons dehydrated bell peppers

3 tablespoons dehydrated spinach

2 vegetable or chicken bouillon cubes, smashed

1/4 teaspoon thyme

1/4 teaspoon freshly ground black pepper plus more to taste

1 shallot

1 tablespoon extra-virgin olive oil

4 cups water

FOR THE DUMPLINGS

1/2 cup all-purpose flour

1 teaspoon baking powder

1/4 teaspoon kosher salt plus more to taste

1 tablespoon butter

1/4 cup water

TOOLS

Backcountry Base Kit

2-liter (or larger) pot with lid

Cutting board (optional)

I spent the entire four months of our trans-Canada bike tour hungry like I had never been before. Kismat was even hungrier than I was, so we would sometimes stop at gas stations mid-morning to buy what we called "pocket snacks" in order to keep him going. I'm pretty sure we doubled our expected food budget. What got me through those long days of cycling was thinking about what I would eat for dinner. I craved all things starchy, and dumplings were often on the menu. Some variation of this recipe was a standard that I came back to over and over again. The dumplings are good for the soul, while the vegetables and lentils nourish the body. You can buy dehydrated lentils online, but they also sell sprouted dried lentils at natural foods stores that cook much quicker than regular dried lentils. —Aimee

AT HOME

In a ziplock bag, combine the dehydrated lentils, bell peppers, spinach, bouillon cubes, thyme, and pepper. In another ziplock bag, combine the flour, baking powder, and salt. In a third ziplock bag, package the butter.

AT CAMP

Chop the shallot. Heat the oil in a pot over medium-high heat. Add shallot and sauté until the shallot is softened, about 5 to 7 minutes. Add the water and the lentil mixture. Bring to a boil, stirring occasionally.

While the stew is coming to a boil, prepare the dumpling dough. Place the butter in the bag with the flour mixture and close the bag. Massage until the mixture resembles coarse crumbs. Then add the water, close the bag, and continue massaging, just until combined.

Using a spoon, scoop tablespoon-sized drops of dough into the stew. Don't worry if they sink to the bottom. Reduce the heat to low and cover the pot with a lid. Simmer for 5 to 10 minutes, until the dumplings are cooked through and vegetables are rehydrated. Season to taste with salt and pepper.

Serving Size: 1/2 the recipe; Calories: 460; Protein: 19 g; Fat: 15 g; Saturated Fat: 4 g; Carbohydrates: 55 g; Fiber: 15 g; Sugar: 1 g

Smoked Salmon and Gravy Mashed Potatoes

Yield: 2 servings

Prep Time: 5 minutes

Cook Time: 5 minutes

2 tablespoons dehydrated spinach

1 (³/₄-ounce) packet mushroom gravy

1 cup unseasoned instant mashed potatoes

1 tablespoon milk powder

2 cups water

1 (8-ounce) smoked salmon fillet

TOOLS

Backcountry Base Kit

I shy away from the popular (read: populated) hiking trails in favor of more obscure areas. My secret is to ask a local ranger what their favorite trail is. This tactic hasn't failed me yet: The trails are always beautiful and worth the risk of showing up sans reservation. One of the standouts was at Mineral King—a long drive out of the way near Sequoia National Park. We did a 60-mile loop that brought us across a range of different ecosystems due to the intense daily elevation changes. We enjoyed many five-star experiences—including Wes's first wild bear sighting—and really worked up an appetite. Due to the length of the trip (six days), weight was an issue, so fully dehydrated meals were aplenty. One of our last nights was spent at Big Arroyo with our offerings down to a variation of these Gravy Mashed Potatoes. Truly, mashed potatoes are a blank canvas to top with all sorts of delicious things and a welcome treat at the end of a long backpacking trip. —*Emily*

AT HOME

In a small ziplock bag, combine spinach and mushroom gravy. In a second small ziplock bag, combine instant potatoes and milk powder.

AT CAMP

In a 1-liter pot, over high heat, add the water, spinach, and mushroom gravy. Bring to a boil. Lower heat and simmer for about 5 minutes.

Meanwhile, break up salmon into big chunks.

Remove pot from heat. Add the potatoes and milk powder to the pot, and mix well.

Serve the mashed potatoes topped with smoked salmon chunks and dig in!

Serving Size: ¹/₂ the recipe; Calories: 360; Protein: 37 g; Fat: 5 g; Saturated Fat: 1 g; Carbohydrates: 39 g; Fiber: 4 g; Sugar: 4 g

Soba Noodles with Sweet Chili Chicken

Yield: 2 servings

Prep Time: 5 minutes

Cook Time: 10 minutes

2 cups water

4 ounces soba noodles

1 tablespoon oil

8 ounces pre-cooked chicken in a foil pouch or can

FOR THE SWEET CHILI SAUCE

1/4 cup freeze-dried scallions

1 tablespoon chili-garlic sauce

1 tablespoon soy sauce

1 tablespoon honey

1 tablespoon rice vinegar

1 tablespoon sesame oil

1 tablespoon sesame seeds

TOOLS

Backcountry Base Kit

7-inch nonstick skillet

I tend to fall in love with certain types of ingredients—usually versatile ones. Soba noodles are one of these ingredients. Healthier and sturdier than ramen, but almost as quick to cook, they can be used in all sorts of recipes—hot, cold, or lukewarm. Canned or foil pouch chicken is a staple in the backcountry, but we like to find ways to make it amazing. Wes and I made Soba Noodles with Sweet Chili Chicken for dinner on a chilly night in Joshua Tree and then ate the leftovers right out of our packs after a few climbs the next day. It's spicy and salty and filling and delicious. —*Emily*

AT HOME

Prepare the sweet chili sauce: In a leak-proof container, combine the scallions, chili-garlic sauce, soy sauce, honey, rice vinegar, sesame oil, and sesame seeds.

AT CAMP

Bring the water to a boil in a pot over high heat. Add the noodles and cook until tender, about 5 minutes. Drain and set aside.

Heat the oil in a skillet over medium-high heat. Add the chicken and sauté until starting to brown, about 5 minutes. Remove from heat. Add the prepared sauce, stirring to coat the chicken. Add saucy chicken to the pot of drained noodles and toss.

Serving Size: 1/2 the recipe; Calories: 530; Protein: 35 g; Fat: 19 g; Saturated Fat: 2 g; Carbohydrates: 55 g; Fiber: 3 g; Sugar: 16 g

Vegetable Fried Rice

Yield: 2 servings

Prep Time: 5 minutes

Cook Time: About 10 minutes

4 tablespoons dehydrated eggs

6 tablespoons mixed dehydrated vegetables, such as peas, carrots, and bell peppers

2 teaspoons brown sugar

½ teaspoon chile flakes

1 cup plus 6 tablespoons water, divided

1 shallot

3 tablespoons vegetable oil, divided

2 (8-ounce) packages cooked rice

2 to-go packets soy sauce (about 2 tablespoons)

3 tablespoons chopped roasted peanuts

Hot sauce

TOOLS

Backcountry Base Kit

Nonstick backpacking skillet

Spatula

2 mugs or small bowls

My dad used to be a mountaineer, but it was mainly before I was born. I spent my childhood hearing tales about his experiences in the High Sierra. As an adult, I've followed in his footsteps to a degree, but it wasn't until Wes and I decided to hike Matterhorn Peak (the Sierra version), that I planned to retrace my dad's actual steps—or so I thought. Dad's excitement was motivating. He had vivid memories of his own trip and gave us a lot of details, except for the most important: he'd done the day-trip version and we were going to backpack in from the opposite side. We'd imagined getting to the summit to find the register still there from when he signed it in the '80s, but by the time we arrived at the knife-edge ridge a second time—and still couldn't find the official summit—we knew it was time to give up. We figured two false summits have to count for something and were happy to have an exciting story of our own. We'd gotten engaged a few weeks before, and so the rest of the trip was spent planning our wedding with our feet in lakes and streams. Vegetable Fried Rice was a new recipe for us on this fateful trip. It's easy and filling and highly recommended for a summit attempt day. —*Emily*

AT HOME

Place the dehydrated eggs in a small ziplock bag. In another small ziplock bag, place the dehydrated vegetables. In a third ziplock bag combine the brown sugar and chile flakes.

AT CAMP

To rehydrate the eggs, pour 6 tablespoons of the water into the ziplock bag of dehydrated eggs. Seal the bag and use your hands to mix together until no large lumps remain.

In a pot over medium heat, bring 1 cup of water to a boil and add the dehydrated vegetables. Remove from heat and set aside to rehydrate the vegetables.

Meanwhile, peel and roughly chop the shallot.

Heat 2 tablespoons of the oil in a skillet over medium-high heat. Add the shallots and sauté until the shallots are softened and slightly caramelized, about 5 minutes. Transfer the shallots to

another container, and set aside. Add the eggs to the hot skillet and scramble. Transfer and set aside with the shallots. Add the remaining 1 tablespoon of oil to the skillet. Add the rice, stirring to coat it in the oil.

Drain the vegetables and add them to the skillet with the rice.

While the rice and vegetables are cooking, combine the soy sauce and brown sugar–chili mixture in a small bowl or mug. Stir to dissolve the sugar.

Once the rice and vegetables are heated through and slightly crispy, stir in the soy sauce mixture and remove from heat. Top the fried rice with fried shallots, eggs, peanuts, and hot sauce.

Serving Size: ¹⁄₂ the recipe; Calories: 790; Protein: 21 g; Fat: 36 g; Saturated Fat: 5 g; Carbohydrates: 163 g; Fiber: 5 g; Sugar: 10 g

Noodles with Spicy Peanut Sauce

Yield: 2 servings

Prep Time: 5 minutes

Cook Time: 10 minutes

6 tablespoons peanut butter powder or regular peanut butter

3 teaspoons brown sugar

2 teaspoons freeze-dried chives

½ teaspoon red chile flakes

¼ teaspoon ginger powder

2 packets ramen or 2 servings of soba noodles

¼ cup dehydrated vegetables, such as green beans, bell peppers, shiitake mushrooms

2 to-go packets of soy sauce (equivalent to 2 tablespoons)

1 lime

4 cups water

TOOLS

Backcountry Base Kit

Mug or second small pot

I first made these noodles after a dip in Kern Hot Spring. While we were soaking, a buck showed up and grazed in the field of wildflowers right next to us. It was literally my dream world. By the time we got back to camp, we were starving and thrilled at how satisfying—and quick-cooking—this peanut butter ramen turned out to be. I shared the recipe with Aimee and Mai-Yan when I got home. Aimee, however, thinks it is worth the weight of an individual peanut butter packet to avoid the peanut butter powder. This is just one of the food debates going on with the three of us at any given time. We'll let you make your own decision about this one. —*Emily*

AT HOME

Prepare the sauce ingredients: In a small ziplock bag, combine the peanut butter powder, brown sugar, chives, chile flakes, and ginger.

Remove the noodles from their packaging and discard the seasoning packet (if included). Place the noodles in a ziplock bag along with the dehydrated vegetables, soy sauce packets, and lime.

Place the small ziplock bag of sauce ingredients inside the larger bag of noodles and vegetables.

AT CAMP

Place the noodles and dehydrated vegetables in a pot and add just enough water to cover them. Bring to a boil. Cook for about 2 minutes, or until the noodles are cooked through and vegetables are rehydrated. Carefully drain the water from the noodles, reserving about ½ cup of the cooking water in a mug.

Into the hot cooking water, add the bag of sauce ingredients and the soy sauce, and stir until ingredients are blended.

Pour the sauce over the noodles and mix well. Finish with a squeeze of lime.

Serving Size: ½ the recipe; Calories: 530; Protein: 19 g; Fat: 16 g; Saturated Fat: 7 g; Carbohydrates: 74 g; Fiber: 5 g; Sugar: 8 g

Panang Curry

Yield: 2 servings

Prep Time: 15 minutes

Cook Time: 15 to 20 minutes

3 tablespoons mixed dehydrated vegetables, such as bell peppers and green beans

1 tablespoon dried onion flakes

2 tablespoons chopped dried mushrooms

$\frac{1}{2}$ cup coconut milk powder

3 tablespoons peanut butter powder

1 teaspoon brown sugar

1 teaspoon garlic powder

$\frac{1}{2}$ teaspoon kosher salt

3 tablespoons red curry paste

$2\frac{3}{4}$ cups water, divided

1 boil-in-bag rice pouch

FOR SERVING

$\frac{1}{2}$ lime, cut into wedges

2 tablespoons chopped peanuts

Red chile flakes

TOOLS

Backcountry Base Kit

Additional $\frac{1}{2}$- to 1-liter pot

The three of us are obsessed with panang curry, thanks to a local restaurant called Mix Bowl. They make the best panang curry we've ever tasted, and we stop in after every trip to Joshua Tree. I decided it was a good recipe to try to replicate in the backcountry on the first trip we went on with our friend Adan. Because he knew me only as "Dirty Gourmet" at that time I wanted to impress him with food. The sauce turned out wonderful, but my rehydrated tofu cubes never rehydrated. Adan ate it anyway, and we've been friends ever since. Mai-Yan took over the recipe, improving the sauce so it's as close to Mix Bowl as you can get without knowing the actual recipe. This is one of the few two-pot recipes in the backcountry section of this book, but it's worth it for this gourmet stick-to-your ribs meal. —*Emily*

AT HOME

In a ziplock bag, combine vegetables, onion flakes and mushrooms. In a second ziplock bag, combine the coconut milk powder, peanut butter powder, brown sugar, garlic powder, and salt. Into a third ziplock bag, measure out curry paste. Tuck the coconut milk and curry paste bags into the vegetable bag.

AT CAMP

Add $\frac{3}{4}$ cup of the water to a small pot and add the vegetables. Bring to a boil over high heat, then remove from heat and set aside to allow the vegetables to rehydrate for about 15 minutes.

Meanwhile, cook the rice. In a large pot over high heat, bring the remaining 2 cups of water to a boil. Add the rice pouch, making sure rice is completely submerged under the water. Boil for 10 minutes, or until rice is tender. Remove the pot from the heat, and carefully pull the rice bag out of the hot water. Holding the perforated rice bag above the pot, let the water drain out and then set rice bag aside. Drain pot water (or save for dirty dishes). Rip top off the rice pouch and pour rice back into the large pot or into individual bowls.

Into the small pot of vegetables, add the coconut milk mixture and the red curry paste, stirring to combine. Return the pot to your stove and cook the curry on medium heat, stirring constantly, until heated through.

Serve curry over rice with a squeeze of lime juice, and top with chopped peanuts and chile flakes.

Serving Size: ¹⁄₂ the recipe; Calories: 530; Protein: 12 g; Fat: 16 g; Saturated Fat: 13 g; Carbohydrates: 82 g; Fiber: 6 g; Sugar: 22 g

African Peanut Soup

Yield: 2 servings
Prep Time: 10 minutes
Cook Time: 15 to 20 minutes

3 vegetable bouillon cubes

2 tablespoons tomato powder

1/4 cup chopped salted peanuts

1 shallot

1 tablespoon extra-virgin olive oil

1 medium sweet potato

1-inch knob of ginger

2 cloves garlic

3 cups water

1 cup chopped kale

2 (1.15-ounce) packets peanut butter (about 1/4 cup)

TOOLS

Backcountry Base Kit

Cutting board (optional)

Our immediate families get sucked into most of our Dirty Gourmet adventures whether they like it or not. Fortunately, they are usually happy to join us. I convinced Kismat to join me on a quick snowshoeing trip near our house to test this recipe for African Peanut Soup. But when it came time to make it, our stove wasn't working properly. We could get it to light, but it wouldn't stay lit unless we continuously pumped it, and the fuel was ever so slowly leaking out of the bottle. It was cold and windy, and I was ready to give up and call it a day, but Kismat sat there and pumped the stove until the soup was done. At least he got a hot meal out of it! —*Aimee*

AT HOME

In a small ziplock bag, combine the bouillon and tomato powder. Place the peanuts in another ziplock bag.

AT CAMP

Dice the shallot and set aside. Dice the sweet potato, and mince the ginger and garlic and set aside.

In a pot over medium-high heat, add the oil and shallot, and sauté the shallot until it is softened, about 5 to 7 minutes. Add the sweet potato, ginger, and garlic, and sauté for 1 minute. Add the water, kale, and bag of bouillon and tomato powder. Stir to combine, cover, and bring to a boil. Reduce the heat to simmer, and cook until the sweet potato is cooked through, about 10 minutes. Stir in the peanut butter and serve, sprinkled with chopped peanuts.

Serving Size: 1/2 the recipe; Calories: 440; Protein: 14 g; Fat: 29 g; Saturated Fat: 5 g; Carbohydrates: 34 g; Fiber: 7 g; Sugar: 7 g

Backcountry Mac and Cheese

Yield: 2 servings

Prep Time: 5 minutes

Cook Time: 15 minutes

5 tablespoons milk powder

4 tablespoons sharp cheddar cheese powder

³/₄ teaspoon freshly ground black pepper

3 tablespoons dried chives

2¹/₂ cups water

2 cups elbow macaroni, uncooked

¹/₂ teaspoon kosher salt

TOOLS

Backcountry Base Kit

Our snow camping turned *snowstorm* backpacking trip in the Los Padres National Forest started with a group of cheery snowshoers setting off down a fire road, but it turned into an off-trail hike into the woods to get out of the blizzard. We stopped early to set up tents and hunker down, but I was determined to keep us warm and together. I found some dry wood under the snow and started a fire, and someone else built us a tarp for shelter. By the end of the night, we'd collectively cooked about twelve different recipes. At the top of the list was this backcountry version of simple perfect mac and cheese. In the morning, Mai-Yan had to dig Aimee and me out of our tent, but it was a bluebird day and we were so happy we'd braved the storm. —*Emily*

Make sure to look at the ingredients in your cheese powder. Some of them contain salt, so you may want to reduce how much salt you add in the recipe.

AT HOME

Prepare the sauce ingredients: In ziplock bag, combine the milk and cheese powders with the pepper. Place the chives in a second small ziplock bag.

AT CAMP

In a 1-liter pot over high heat, combine water, macaroni, and salt, bringing to a boil. Reduce heat to medium-low, and continue to cook, stirring often, until macaroni is al dente, about 10 minutes. There should still be water left in the pot. Add the sauce ingredients and continue to stir and simmer for another 5 minutes. Remove from heat and stir in the chives.

Serving Size: ¹/₂ the recipe; Calories: 590; Protein: 23 g; Fat: 12 g; Saturated Fat: 6 g; Carbohydrates: 92 g; Fiber: 4 g; Sugar: 11 g

Cheesy Mountain Ramen

Yield: 2 servings

Prep Time: 5 minutes

Cook Time: 5 minutes

1 to 2 small bouillon cubes, flavor of your choice

2 (10-gram) instant miso soup packets

½ cup freeze-dried corn

8 dried shiitake mushrooms, broken in small pieces and stem discarded

2 to 4 ounces spicy beef jerky (or flavor of your choice), torn in bite-sized pieces

½ cup Parmesan cheese, grated

4 cups water

2 packages instant ramen noodle soup

TOOLS

Backcountry Base Kit

After expressing some interest in the outdoors, my friends Beth and Joyce prompted a backpacking trip for their maiden voyage into the wild with me as their guide. Although I had many years of backpacking under my belt, I felt a lot of pressure as a first-time trip leader. It was a test of my skills and my confidence: providing gear advice, researching the most appropriate route, acquiring a permit, meal planning, etc. I fretted even up to the point we hopped into the car ready to hit the road. Despite it being a busy holiday weekend, we had the trail to ourselves. Their full trust in me and easygoing attitudes helped validate my skill set and boost my confidence—something that I really needed at that point in my life. My other reward was using them as recipe guinea pigs making this "dressed-up" version of instant noodles. I replaced the MSG flavor packet with a miso soup base and topped it all off with a mountain of Parmesan cheese. It sounds crazy, but it's delicious. —*Mai-Yan*

AT HOME

Break up the bouillon cubes into small pieces and combine with the miso soup packet contents, corn, and mushrooms in a ziplock bag. In a second ziplock bag, combine Parmesan and jerky.

AT CAMP

Put the water in a small pot. Add the bouillon–dehydrated vegetable mixture and bring to a boil. When the water is boiling, add the noodles and simmer until noodles start to get soft, about 3 minutes. Remove from the heat and top soup with Parmesan cheese and beef jerky. Carefully eat straight out of the pot using your bandana as a trivet.

Serving Size: ½ the recipe; Calories: 660; Protein: 36 g; Fat: 26 g; Saturated Fat: 13 g; Carbohydrates: 73 g; Fiber: 5 g; Sugar: 88 g

Rice Bowls with Creamy Italian Dressing

Yield: 2 servings

Prep Time: 10 minutes

Cook Time: 10 minutes

2 cups water

1 boil-in-bag rice pouch

1 red bell pepper, chopped

1 avocado, chopped

¼ cup chopped almonds

¼ cup chopped or shredded beef jerky

FOR THE DRESSING

3 tablespoons milk powder

1 teaspoon dried onion

½ teaspoon garlic powder

½ teaspoon Italian seasoning

½ teaspoon kosher salt

½ teaspoon freshly ground black pepper

¼ to ½ cup water

Juice of 1 lemon

FOR THE SEED DUST

2 tablespoons pepitas

2 tablespoons sunflower seeds

1 tablespoon sesame seeds

TOOLS

Backcountry Base Kit

Mug or small bowl

Cutting board

Hiking in the backcountry makes bringing fresh ingredients a little tricky, because we want our packs as light as possible. But river trips, like the kayaking trip I took down the Suwannee River with my best friend, Anne, take some of these worries away. We floated the whole way downstream, giving us plenty of energy to jump off bridges, instigate paddle battles, and run around exploring dry land each evening. One of the paddle battles resulted in a rafting colony of fire ants being flung at my head. They cling together while in water (looking something like a natural sponge, so says Anne), but as soon as they hit dry land (or dry human), they disperse and grab on to whatever they can. I survived with minimal injury—and Anne now owes me *for life*. These rice bowls can be adapted to include as many or as few fresh ingredients as your trip will allow. The ingredients listed here are sturdy enough for most adventures. —*Emily*

AT HOME

First, make the seed dust. In a clean coffee grinder or small food processor, add the pepitas, sunflower seeds, and sesame seeds, and grind for about 10 seconds. Keep this as crumbly and crunchy as you like. If you go too far, it will begin to turn into a paste. Store the mixture in a ziplock bag.

Next, make the dressing mix. In a second ziplock bag, combine the milk powder, dried onion, garlic powder, Italian seasoning, salt, and pepper.

AT CAMP

In a pot over high heat, bring water to a boil. Add the rice pouch, making sure rice is completely submerged under the water. Boil for 10 minutes, or until rice is tender.

Meanwhile, make the dressing. To the bag of dry ingredients, add ¼ cup of water and lemon juice, stirring to combine. (Alternately, you can use a mug or small bowl to mix these ingredients). Let sit about 5 minutes.

Remove the pot from the heat, and carefully pull the rice bag out of the hot water. Holding the perforated rice bag above the pot,

let the water drain out and then set rice bag aside. Drain pot water (or save for dirty dishes). Rip top off the rice pouch and pour rice back into the large pot or into individual bowls. Top rice with bell pepper, avocado, almonds, and jerky. Sprinkle with the seed dust.

Check dressing for consistency, adding a little more water to thin it out, if desired. Pour dressing over rice bowl and enjoy.

Serving Size: 1/2 the recipe; Calories: 640; Protein: 25 g; Fat: 32 g; Saturated Fat: 5 g; Carbohydrates: 87 g; Fiber: 16 g; Sugar: 21 g

Walnut and Almond Tacos

Yield: 2 servings

Prep Time: 5 minutes

Cook Time: 5 minutes

1/3 cup toasted walnuts

1/3 cup toasted almonds

1/4 cup drained oil-packed sun-dried tomatoes

2 teaspoons soy sauce

1 teaspoon balsamic vinegar

1/2 teaspoon garlic powder

1/2 teaspoon smoked paprika

1/4 teaspoon cumin

Pinch of cayenne pepper

1 carrot

1 avocado

6 (4-inch) corn or flour tortillas

FOR SERVING (OPTIONAL)

Hot sauce

1 lime

TOOLS

Backcountry Base Kit

Skillet for warming tortillas (optional)

I was invited to go on a backpacking trip to Little Lakes Valley Trail in the eastern Sierra Nevada that was put together by and for women entrepreneurs and influencers in the outdoor industry. Even though going on a trip with a bunch of strangers is completely out of my comfort zone, I signed up, lured by the promise of one of the most beautiful trails in California. It turned out to be an amazing trip, where we all shared vulnerable conversations. This recipe is adapted from my favorite meal from that trip, prepared by a lovely woman named Julie. Ground walnuts and almonds act as the *meat* in these tacos, so it's a healthy filling. Bulk up this meal even further by serving the tacos with some rehydrated black bean flakes, either on the side or in the tacos. The carrot and avocado are totally optional, but I think they're worth the weight! —*Aimee*

AT HOME

In a food processor fitted with the metal blade attachment, place the walnuts, almonds, sun-dried tomatoes, soy sauce, vinegar, garlic powder, paprika, cumin, and cayenne. Process until the nuts and sun-dried tomatoes are finely chopped, but be careful not to process too long so you don't end up with a paste. Package the nut meat in a ziplock bag.

AT CAMP

Finely chop or shred the carrot and set aside. Slice the avocado and set aside.

Heat the tortillas in a skillet or directly over the flame of the stove.

Divide the nut meat between the tortillas and top with the prepared carrot and avocado. Serve immediately with hot sauce and a squeeze of lime, if desired.

Serving Size: 1/2 the recipe; Calories: 590; Protein: 14 g; Fat: 40 g; Saturated Fat: 4 g; Carbohydrates: 51 g; Fiber: 15 g; Sugar: 7 g

French Onion Chicken Noodles

Yield: 2 servings

Prep Time: 10 minutes

Cook Time: 10 to 12 minutes

¼ cup freeze-dried peas

⅛ cup dehydrated carrots

½ cup of crispy French fried onions

6 ounces wide egg noodles

3 cups of water

1 (5-ounce) can of white chicken

FOR THE SAUCE

5 tablespoons sour cream powder

2 tablespoons powdered Parmesan (optional)

2 teaspoons cornstarch

1 (0.5-ounce) packet toasted onion dip (or French onion dip)

½ teaspoon onion powder

½ teaspoon kosher salt

¼ teaspoon freshly ground black pepper

¼ teaspoon garlic powder

TOOLS

Backcountry Base Kit

This dish is a cross between Mom's casserole, your favorite high school–era chip dip, and Thanksgiving dinner. It is a heavy-duty meal best reserved for the night before a *big* day. The use of egg noodles adds extra protein to the dish in addition to the healthy amount of chicken. The whole dish hinges on a pepper cream sauce that is topped with crispy French fried onions (yes, the same ones used for green bean casserole). This carbo-loading feast will fuel you into the next day and guarantee a good night of sleep. —*Mai-Yan*

AT HOME

In a small ziplock bag, combine sour cream powder, Parmesan, cornstarch, onion dip, onion powder, salt, pepper, and garlic powder.

In a second small ziplock bag, place the peas and carrots. In a third ziplock bag, place the fried onions. In a large ziplock bag, measure out egg noodles. Tuck the three small ziplock bags into the large bag.

AT CAMP

In a mug, soak the peas and carrots in ½ cup of water for at least 10 minutes.

In a small pot, add the remaining water, egg noodles, peas and carrots (with soaking water), and stir. (The water will not quite cover the noodles and that is OK.) Bring mixture to a boil, then lower heat to a simmer, stirring often. When noodles are just shy of al dente, about 5 minutes, add the sauce ingredients and stir immediately. Lower the flame and gently stir pasta continuously until sauce thickens and noodles are cooked, about 2 minutes. Remove from the heat, stir in the chicken, and top with the fried onions.

Serving Size: ½ the recipe; Calories: 720; Protein: 38 g; Fat: 25 g; Saturated Fat: 9 g; Carbohydrates: 83 g; Fiber: 6 g; Sugar: 12 g

Blackened Trout Tacos with Spicy Slaw

Yield: 2 servings

Prep Time: 20 minutes

Cook Time: 15 minutes

2 fresh-caught trout

4 (10.6-gram) mayonnaise condiment packets

Juice of 1 lime

1 tablespoon hot sauce

2 tablespoons oil

8 (5-inch) corn tortillas

1 cup shredded cabbage

FOR THE SPICE MIX

2 teaspoons smoked paprika

2 teaspoons cumin

$\frac{1}{2}$ teaspoon onion powder

$\frac{1}{2}$ teaspoon garlic powder

$\frac{1}{2}$ teaspoon kosher salt

$\frac{1}{2}$ teaspoon pepper

$\frac{1}{8}$ teaspoon cayenne pepper

TOOLS

Backcountry Base Kit

7-inch nonstick skillet or foil pouch

Spatula

Small bowl or mug

My dream scenario is heading out to the backcountry far from other humans on a perfect summer day, spending the daylight hours fishing and creating a delicious dinner out of the fresh catch. There are a lot of amazing places to do this. I have awesome childhood memories of camping with Aimee's family in Dinkey Lakes Wilderness, jumping and sliding off rocks into ice-cold pools and casting our lines directly at the fish because the water was so clear. Once, I caught a fish with my bare hands, impressing Aimee's brother who was trying to whittle himself a spear. This sort of setting is an ideal way to discover and enjoy self-reliance and to understand the connection we all have to the earth and each other. —*Emily*

AT HOME

Prepare the spice mix: In a ziplock bag, combine the paprika, cumin, onion powder, garlic powder, salt, pepper, and cayenne.

AT CAMP

Catch and clean the fish. Season the cavity with a big pinch of the spice mix, and set aside.

In a small bowl, combine the mayonnaise, lime juice, and hot sauce. Stir to combine.

Heat the oil in a skillet over medium heat, and pan fry the fish (or cook in a foil pouch in a fire), until meat is opaque and flaky, about 10 minutes. Remove from the heat. Strip the meat and skin from the skeleton. Set aside.

In a skillet or directly over the flame of the stove, heat the tortillas, flipping quickly a few times until heated through.

Assemble each taco with fish in the middle, and top with the cabbage and the prepared lime-mayonnaise sauce.

Serving Size: $\frac{1}{2}$ the recipe; Calories: 520; Protein: 24 g; Fat: 27 g; Saturated Fat: 3 g; Carbohydrates: 49 g; Fiber: 8 g; Sugar: 6 g

Masala Chai

Yield: About 4 drinks

Prep Time: 5 minutes

Cook Time: 5 minutes

FOR THE MIX

3 tablespoons milk powder

2 tablespoons sugar

$\frac{1}{2}$ teaspoon ground ginger

$\frac{1}{4}$ teaspoon ground cardamom

$\frac{1}{4}$ teaspoon freshly ground black pepper

$\frac{1}{4}$ teaspoon ground cinnamon

FOR CHAI AT CAMP

4 bags black tea

TOOLS

Backcountry Base Kit

Mug

I don't think there's a wrong or right way to make chai. It's highly personal, and recipes are often passed down in Indian families. Here's my backpacking version. If it doesn't warm you from the inside out, I'm not sure what will. Play with the quantities of each spice and the sugar to suit your tastes. This one has a kick from the black pepper and ginger—what makes chai delicious to my taste buds—but tame it by reducing these ingredients, if you like. Either way, be sure to use a good, strong black tea. —*Aimee*

AT HOME

In a small bowl, combine the milk powder, sugar, ginger, cardamom, pepper, and cinnamon. Mix well to combine. Pack in a ziplock.

AT CAMP

To make 1 cup of chai, measure out the water needed by filling your mug.

Place a pot over high heat, add the water, 1 tea bag, and 1 tablespoon of the masala chai mix. Stir to combine and bring to a boil. Boil for about 2 minutes, then remove the tea bag and taste, adding additional chai mix to taste. Serve immediately.

Serving Size: 1 cup; Calories: 50; Protein: 2 g; Fat: 2 g; Saturated Fat: 1 g; Carbohydrates: 8 g; Fiber: 0 g; Sugar: 8 g

Coconut Matcha Latte

Yield: 1 serving
Prep Time: 2 minutes
Cook Time: 2 minutes

¼ cup coconut milk powder

1 teaspoon matcha powder

2 to 3 teaspoons sweetener, such as honey powder, maple sugar, or granulated sugar

TOOLS

Backcountry Base Kit

Mug

Matcha is one of my favorite ways to get a nice mild caffeine buzz in the backcountry. It is finely ground green tea that dissolves in water so there's no dealing with packing out coffee grinds or tea leaves. It has a strong green tea flavor, so the fat in the coconut milk powder and some sweetener help to round out the flavor. I like this with two teaspoons of sugar, but experiment at home before your trip to figure out how much sweetener you like. Matcha powder can be found in many regular markets nowadays, but if you can't find it near you, it can also be purchased online. —*Aimee*

AT HOME

Using a fine mesh sieve, sift both powders together to break up as many lumps as possible. Pour the mixture and the sweetener into a ziplock bag.

AT CAMP

To make 1 cup, measure out the water needed by filling your mug. Pour it into a pot and bring to a boil over high heat.

Meanwhile, pour the matcha powder mixture into the mug, using your fingers to break up any lumps. Pour a couple tablespoons of boiling water into the mug and use a spork to stir the mixture until you have a slurry, or smooth green paste.

Add the remaining water, stir well, and serve immediately.

Serving Size: 1 cup; Calories: 230; Protein: 1 g; Fat: 14 g; Saturated Fat: 13 g; Carbohydrates: 24 g; Fiber: 0 g; Sugar: 24 g

COCONUT MATCHA LATTE

HIBISCUS CHIA COOLER (PG 240)

Hibiscus Chia Cooler

Yield: 1 serving

Prep Time: 5 minutes

Cook Time: 10 minutes

2 tablespoons dried hibiscus flowers

2 tablespoons sugar

½ teaspoon dried mint

¼ teaspoon cinnamon

1 tablespoon chia seeds

2 cups water

TOOLS

Backcountry Base Kit

Reusable bottle

I'm one of those people who hates to drink water. I'll force myself to chug a bunch at once to stay hydrated, but I'm not one for sipping throughout the day. If, however, my drink is a glorious shade of pink and a little bit sweet, that changes everything. The color of this drink is bright, but the flavor is subtle. Chia seeds give it a little interest and some extra protein. I like to make this the night before so it has a chance to chill and the chia seeds become a more plump, drinkable texture. —*Aimee*

AT HOME

Combine hibiscus flowers, sugar, mint, and cinnamon in a small ziplock bag.

Place the chia seeds in another small ziplock bag and tuck this bag into the other.

AT CAMP

In a pot, bring 2 cups of water to a boil over high heat. Remove from heat and stir in the hibiscus mixture. Let steep for about 5 minutes, and then carefully strain the tea into a bottle. Add the chia seeds, close the bottle and shake to combine. Let sit for at least 1 hour so that the chia seeds can absorb some liquid.

Serving Size: 1 recipe; Calories: 210; Protein: 3 g; Fat: 3 g; Saturated Fat: 1 g; Carbohydrates: 44 g; Fiber: 10 g; Sugar: 32 g

Gin and Jam

Yield: 1 cocktail

Prep Time: 1 minute

1½ ounces gin
1 teaspoon jam
1 lime wedge

TOOLS

Backcountry Base Kit
Cup

We named this cocktail after my parents, Ginny and James, who were with us camping when we made it up. It's an ultralight drink for a cool evening surrounded by wildflowers and requires only three ingredients that are probably already in your pack anyway. A single-serve jam packet from a diner works well, and is enough to make two drinks. This drink may be shot sized, but it should be sipped. —*Emily*

Squeeze the jam into the bottom of a cup. Pour in the gin, and swirl or stir to mix. Squeeze in lime. Sip. You can go one step further and chill the gin in a mountain stream or snowpack ahead of time, if available.

Serving Size: 1 cocktail; Calories: 130; Protein: 0 g; Fat: 0 g; Saturated Fat: 0 g; Carbohydrates: 5 g; Fiber: 0 g; Sugar: 4 g

Blueberry Hot Toddy

Yield: 2 servings

Prep Time: 20 minutes, inactive

Cook Time: 1 minute

¼ cup dried blueberries

⅓ cup whiskey

1½ cups water

2 teaspoons maple sugar, brown sugar, or honey

1 small lemon, cut into wedges, for serving

TOOLS

Backcountry Base Kit

Mugs

Soaking dried blueberries in whiskey not only rehydrates the berries, but it also infuses the whiskey with blueberry flavor, turning it a deep purple color with a thick, syrupy consistency. Wrap up your long day of adventure with a cozy hot toddy, and get an antioxidant boost from the blueberries! —*Aimee*

Combine the blueberries and whiskey in a small pot, and bring to a simmer over medium heat. Remove from the heat and set aside for at least 15 minutes to allow the blueberries to infuse the whiskey and to rehydrate. Add the water and sugar, and return the pot to high heat, bringing the mixture to a simmer.

Divide mixture into two mugs, and serve with a squeeze and wedge of lemon.

Serving Size: ½ the recipe; Calories: 170; Protein: 1 g; Fat: 0 g; Saturated Fat: 0 g; Carbohydrates: 20 g; Fiber: 3 g; Sugar: 10 g

Lemongrass Lime Sake Cocktail

Yield: 1 cocktail
Prep Time: 2 minutes
Cook Time: 5 minutes

2 tablespoons lemongrass, chopped
1 tablespoon sugar
³/₄ cup sake
¼ cup water
1 lime

TOOLS

Backcountry Base Kit
Cup

It has been said that sake doesn't cause hangovers. This makes it a perfect drink for the backcountry when you have to get up at 4:00 AM the next day to start hiking or climbing. Plus, you can drink it hot. Here's an easy hot sake cocktail to warm you up. The weight of your pack can muddle your lemongrass throughout the day, readying it to give off a beautiful fragrance when it's time. Lemongrass has a tough texture and is not easily chewable, but the chopped pieces in your drink will sink, so they shouldn't get in your way. Feel free to strain them off if you prefer. —*Emily*

AT HOME

Combine the lemongrass and sugar in a small ziplock bag, scaling the amount per number of drinks planned. Stick it at the bottom of your bear canister or pack so the ingredients get muddled together.

AT CAMP

Into a pot over medium-low heat, bring sake, water, and lemongrass-sugar mixture to a simmer, then remove from heat and let stand for 5 minutes to further infuse the lemongrass flavor. Reheat if desired, depending on the weather.

Pour sake into a cup and add a squeeze of lime.

Serving Size: 1 cocktail; Calories: 190; Protein: 1 g; Fat: 0 g; Saturated Fat: 0 g; Carbohydrates: 23 g; Fiber: 0 g; Sugar: 19 g

DESSERTS

Churro Chocodillas

Yield: 4 servings

Prep Time: 2 minutes

Cook Time: 8 minutes

2 tablespoons sugar

1½ teaspoons cinnamon

4 teaspoons coconut oil

4 (6-inch) flour tortillas

4 heaping tablespoons chocolate chips

TOOLS

Backcountry Base Kit

Skillet

Spatula

One of my complaints about backpacking food is that it's often mushy and served in a bowl—or, straight out of the pot. So, if I'm going to bother with making a dessert, I want it to include some texture and variety to counterbalance all the bowl meals. These Churro Chocodillas are crispy on the outside and gooey on the inside, and they totally satisfy both my sweet tooth and my desire for variety on the trail. —*Aimee*

AT HOME

Combine the sugar and cinnamon in a small ziplock bag.

AT CAMP

Heat about 1 teaspoon of the oil in a skillet over high heat. Place a tortilla in the skillet and sprinkle half the tortilla with about 1 tablespoon of the chocolate chips. Fold over the tortilla and brown lightly on each side, about 2 minutes. Remove from heat and sprinkle with cinnamon-sugar mixture. Cut into a few triangles, and serve immediately. Repeat with the remaining tortillas.

Serving Size: 1 chocodilla; Calories: 230; Protein: 4 g; Fat: 10 g; Saturated Fat: 7 g; Carbohydrates: 31 g; Fiber: 2 g; Sugar: 15 g

Chocolate Berry Fondue

Yield: 2 servings

Prep Time: 5 minutes

Cook Time: 5 minutes

1 tablespoon berry jam (strawberry, blackberry, or raspberry are all nice)

1.4 ounces dark chocolate, broken into pieces

1½ cups water

Shortbread cookies

TOOLS

Backcountry Base Kit

Aluminum foil

I've held a lot of jobs in my life, but one of the most challenging ones was as the "chef" to a group of twelve industry people on an overnight bike-packing trip. It sounds fancy and exciting, but in reality, I was new to riding a fat bike and had little trail riding experience. I was nervous! The ride started in Boulder City, Nevada, and took us across the scenic Hoover Dam, ending in Arizona at a "campsite" next to the Colorado River. The plan was for a couple people to kayak down the river and leave us a secret stash of goods, including coffee, firewood, and the fresh berries for this recipe. I was going to impress this crew with a three-course meal. Well, by the time we arrived, it was close to midnight, I was suffering from severe dehydration, and the secret stash was nowhere to be found. Fortunately, everyone survived, but the berry fondue never happened. I've since concocted this new and improved version. The best part is that it doesn't require a secret stash. —*Mai-Yan*

AT HOME

Make an origami aluminum foil bowl (see the Appendix for instructions). Pack it in a safe place to avoid a leaky bowl.

AT CAMP

Pry open the top of the aluminum foil bowl, and gently push in the bottom to create a base. Add the jam and chocolate to the bowl, and set aside.

In a pot over high heat, bring the water to a rolling boil. Remove from heat.

Hold the aluminum foil bowl upright into the hot water and stir the mixture gently until the chocolate melts. The bottom of the bowl should be resting on top of the hot water rather than submerged. Remove the bowl from the water and use the hot water to make a cup of tea.

Serve fondue immediately with shortbread cookies.

Serving Size: ½ the recipe; Calories: 280; Protein: 3 g; Fat: 14 g; Saturated Fat: 7 g; Carbohydrates: 39 g; Fiber: 2 g; Sugar: 23 g

Cardamom Rice Pudding

Yield: 2 servings
Prep Time: 5 minutes
Cook Time: 15 minutes

³/₄ cup instant rice

4 tablespoons milk powder, preferably full fat

1 tablespoon plus 2 teaspoons sugar

1 teaspoon vanilla powder

¹/₄ teaspoon ground cardamom

1 cup water

TOOLS

Backcountry Base Kit

After college, Kismat and I lived in Finland for a couple of years, and there began my fixation on cardamom. At every corner shop, you could find delicious, lightly sweetened breads flecked with cardamom and topped with pearl sugar. I ate one almost every day, and if I still lived there today I'm sure all my pants would sport elastic waistbands. While the breads were my favorite, Kismat loved the cardamom-scented rice pudding sold at the grocery store that came in little yogurt-sized containers. Puddings are a pretty common backpacking dessert since they don't require baking, and sometimes not even cooking. You *will* need to take out your stove for this recipe, but it's quick and easy. The addition of cardamom makes it exotic, but it's still total comfort food. —*Aimee*

AT HOME

Place the rice in a ziplock bag. In another ziplock bag, combine milk powder, sugar, vanilla powder, and cardamom.

AT CAMP

In a pot over high heat, bring the water to a rolling boil, and then adjust the stove to the lowest setting possible. Add the milk powder mixture, and stir until no lumps remain. Immediately add rice, and stir constantly for about 2 minutes. Remove from heat and cover the pot for 10 minutes. Stir again and serve.

Serving Size: ¹/₂ the recipe; Calories: 250; Protein: 7 g; Fat: 5 g; Saturated Fat: 3 g; Carbohydrates: 43 g; Fiber: 1 g; Sugar: 16 g

Rocky Road Chia Pudding

Yield: 2 servings

Prep Time: 5 minutes, plus 20 minutes to set the pudding

1½ cups water, divided

2 tablespoons coconut milk powder

2 teaspoons cocoa powder

¼ cup chia seeds

2 tablespoons maple sugar

FOR SERVING

Mini marshmallows

Chocolate shavings

Chopped toasted almonds

TOOLS

Backcountry Base Kit

Chia seeds have been made popular in recent years thanks to their superfood qualities. We try to avoid getting caught up in trends but have settled on loving this ingredient for backpacking anyway. Chia seeds thicken to a jelly-like consistency when added to liquid, making them a good non-perishable egg substitute in day trip and backcountry recipes. *This* recipe uses chia seeds as the main event. If, like me, rocky road is your favorite ice cream flavor, then you'll find Rocky Road Chia Pudding a great stand-in while in the wild. —*Emily*

AT HOME

Combine the milk powder and cocoa powder in a small ziplock bag. In another ziplock bag, combine the chia seeds and maple sugar. Tuck one inside the other, and seal.

AT CAMP

In a pot or bowl, add about ½ cup water with the milk and cocoa powder. Mix to make a slurry. Add the remaining 1 cup of water, along with the chia seeds and maple sugar, and mix well. Let the mixture sit for at least 20 minutes, preferably somewhere cool, until chia seeds are plump and jelly-like.

Divide into individual serving bowls or mugs, and serve topped with marshmallows, chocolate shavings, and toasted almonds.

Serving Size: ½ the recipe; Calories: 290; Protein: 11 g; Fat: 18 g; Saturated Fat: 7 g; Carbohydrates: 27 g; Fiber: 13 g; Sugar: 12 g

Chocolate Peanut Butter Fudge

Yield: About 10 pieces

Prep Time: 2 minutes

Cook Time: 2 minutes

$^{2}/_{3}$ cup powdered sugar

2 tablespoons chocolate chips

$^{1}/_{3}$ cup natural style peanut butter, well mixed

2 tablespoons coconut oil

Pinch of kosher salt, plus more to finish

TOOLS

Backcountry Base Kit

Unless you're a scout or on a guided mountaineering trip, you're unlikely to be traveling in large numbers in the backcountry. After a too-long stint in the city, the mountains were calling—urgently—so Daniel and I agreed to join a group of twelve people we barely knew to go to Summit Lake in the Sierra Nevada. We hiked through lush green meadows, conquered leg-numbing river crossings, and post-holed our way across the melting snowpack. Once settled in at camp, stories and food were generously shared leading to a great weekend of exploring, alpine lake fishing, and lazy afternoon hammock naps. It was a real adventure. It's important to remember wilderness is a great retreat from the city, but it doesn't mean you can't enjoy it with others. For such occasions, make this decadent fudge recipe, which is portioned to share. You never know, you may acquire some lifelong friends. —*Mai-Yan*

AT HOME

Into a small bowl, sift the powdered sugar to get rid of any lumps. Pack it in a ziplock bag. Pack the chocolate chips in a separate ziplock bag.

AT CAMP

In a 1-liter pot over medium-high heat, combine the peanut butter and coconut oil and heat until the mixture is completely melted. Remove from heat and stir in the powdered sugar until the sugar is completely mixed in. It should be thick like cookie dough.

Immediately spread out the mixture in an even layer in the bottom of the pot. Sprinkle with the chocolate chips and let the chocolate melt for about 1 minute. Then, use a spork or other utensil to swirl through the fudge and chocolate to create a marble effect. Set aside in a cool place until the fudge hardens. Slice the fudge into small pieces and serve.

Serving Size: 1 piece; Calories: 120; Protein: 2 g; Fat: 8 g; Saturated Fat: 4 g; Carbohydrates: 11 g; Fiber: 1 g; Sugar: 9 g

Pineapple Rum Pudding Parfaits

Yield: 2 servings
Prep Time: 5 minutes
Cook Time: 1 minute

1/4 cup dry milk powder

1.7 ounces instant vanilla pudding mix (equivalent to two servings)

2 cups water, divided

1 ounce freeze-dried or dried pineapple

2 tablespoons rum

About 16 vanilla wafers

TOOLS

Backcountry Base Kit

2 bowls or mugs

On our bike tour, Mai-Yan and I could barely finish a beer without feeling drunk. While it might sound like a nice way to wind down after a long day of pedaling, sometimes alcohol is just too much for a tired, dehydrated body. These Pineapple Rum Pudding Parfaits include a little bit of rum—just enough to feel like a celebration, but not enough to drag you down after a long day. I like to think of it as a boozy tropical take on banana pudding. —*Aimee*

AT HOME

Combine milk powder with pudding mix in a ziplock bag, and mix well.

AT CAMP

Bring 1 cup of the water to a boil in a small pot over high heat. Remove from heat and then add the pineapple. Set aside.

Now prepare the pudding: Add the remaining 1 cup of the water into the pudding mixture bag. Seal the bag, removing the air, and massage the mixture until it's well mixed and there are no lumps. Set aside.

Drain as much water as you can from the pineapple and then stir in the rum.

Layer components into two bowls, first layering the vanilla wafers, then the rum-soaked pineapple, and finally the pudding. You can make two or three layers in each bowl, depending on size. Set aside for at least 15 minutes in a cool place.

Serving Size: 1/2 the recipe; Calories: 250; Protein: 4 g; Fat: 5 g; Saturated Fat: 3 g; Carbohydrates: 40 g; Fiber: 2 g; Sugar: 38 g

APPENDIX

Here we offer a few of our "tricks of the trade" to help make things easier while you perfect the art of campfire cooking. If you're using foil pouches, be sure to tuck an extra roll of foil into your camping bin so you don't run out mid-prep!

HOW TO MAKE AN ALUMINUM FOIL POUCH

Many of our campfire recipes require cooking in an aluminum foil pouch. It's simple and there are no dishes to deal with after the meal. The key to making a good foil pouch is to have a lot of extra foil. Make sure there is extra room around the contents of the pouch so heat can build up inside the pouch creating a mini-oven condition. The worst thing that can happen is the foil pouch falling open as you are handling it because it is overfilled. Don't be responsible for ruining dinner!

THE BASICS:

• Minimum length to make a proper foil pouch: 12 inches.

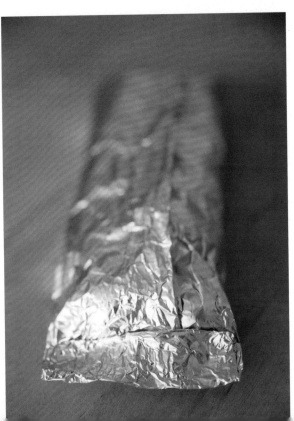

STEP 1

- Splurge on the heavy-duty aluminum foil. It's worth it!
- Use long-handled tongs to transport foil pouches in and out of the fire.

THE DIRECTIONS:

1. Find a flat surface to work on and pull out a sheet of aluminum foil at least 12 inches long.
2. Place your food directly in the center of the foil pouch. Add oil and seasonings if you haven't already done so.
3. Hold the two long edges of foil and bring together in the center above the food. (If your piece of aluminum foil is more like a square, choose the side that is facing you to keep things simple.)
4. Fold the edges down creating a small lip—about ½ inch along the entire length of the foil. Make sure there is room between the food and the foil (1½ to 2 inches) so heat can build up inside the packet.
5. Fold the lip over so it lies flat on top of the foil pouch. The top of the foil pouch should now be sealed leaving two open "short" edges.
6. Press the short edges together and fold over once to create another ½-inch lip. Again, make sure there is plenty of room between the food and the edge of the foil.
7. Fold the lip over so it lies flat on top of the foil pouch. The foil packet should now be tightly sealed on all sides and stay closed when you handle it.
8. Handle the foil pouch along the folded edges (where there are several layers of foil) rather than the middle (where the foil can easily tear with a jab from your tongs).

STEP 2

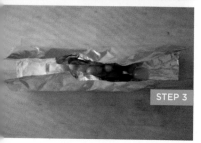

STEP 3

STEP 4

STEP 5

STEPS 6-7

Tips for adding food to the pouch: Plan to add all of your contents at once, since it is not easy to open the pouch multiple times during the cooking process. You want to choose items that don't require a lot of stirring. Also, expect a little char. Since this material is one of the thinnest options, the food will cook quickly and probably a little unevenly unless you move it around consistently. That's OK, and adds a lot of flavor to things like roasted peppers or chicken. Enjoy the campfire flavor!

HOW TO MAKE AN ORIGAMI ALUMINUM FOIL BOWL

Origami craft time! It is really easy to make an aluminum foil bowl and should take you five minutes, tops. This is a necessary step for making our delicious Chocolate Berry Fondue recipe (see Backcountry Camping, Desserts) but is a handy trick to have in your back pocket when you need a bowl in a pinch (enjoying trail mix without spilling in the woods or sharing your water bottle with the dog).

1. Cut a length of aluminum foil roughly equal to the height of the sheet. (You're aiming for as close to a square as possible.)
2. Fold foil in half to make a triangle.
3. Fold the top corner of triangle down so that the right edges meet the bottom edge. Press down to crease and then unfold.
4. Fold the right bottom corner up so its tip meets the left edge of the foil at the creased line.
5. Next, fold the bottom left corner up so it meets the corner you just created.
6. Fold the top flap down toward you. Fold the other flap down to the back side.

If you're prepping this at home, leave the bowl flat until you're ready to use it, and make sure to pack it in a spot where it won't get ripped.

DUTCH OVEN BAKING CHARCOAL CHART

Dutch Oven Size			BAKING TEMPERATURE (°F)					
			325°	350°	375°	400°	425°	450°
			Numbers of Charcoals Needed*					
8"	TOTAL		15	16	17	18	19	20
	On Lid		10	11	11	12	13	14
	Bottom		5	5	6	6	6	6
10"	TOTAL		19	21	23	25	27	29
	On Lid		13	14	16	17	18	19
	Bottom		6	7	7	8	9	10
12"	TOTAL		23	25	27	29	31	33
	On Lid		16	17	18	19	21	22
	Bottom		7	8	9	10	10	11
14"	TOTAL		30	32	34	36	38	40
	On Lid		20	21	22	24	25	26
	Bottom		10	11	12	12	13	14

* Based on standard-size charcoal briquettes.

ACKNOWLEDGMENTS

Making this book was the most intensive project we've done so far. We could not have done it without our family and friends who willingly ate many variations of each recipe, sometimes all in the same day, and put up with kitchens and garages stacked high with ingredients and camping gear. Daniel Pouliot was indispensable for his photography skills, and Wes Nielson for his eagerness to test our recipes on all of his climbing and hiking trips. Kismat Sood and Linda Trudeau patiently chased twin toddlers around while we tested as many recipes as daylight would allow. Virginia Trudeau even spent her birthday dragging her full studio setup around the wilderness to get our headshots. We also need to thank Billie and Adan Lopez for the beautiful dishware and linens they donated to the cause, the Adventure Scouts crew for all the recipe feedback, and Ryan Miller, who taught us so much about food styling and photography. We couldn't have done it without them all, and hope everyone is as fortunate as we are to have such excellent folks around to support their dreams.

INDEX

ABOUT *dirty* GOURMET

Emily spent spring break 2009 visiting her cousin Aimee in San Diego, sleeping in the spare bedroom next to a couple of loaded touring bikes. Aimee was preparing for a summertime bike trip with her friend Mai-Yan that would take them up the California coast to Canada and all the way across to Montreal. Emily was finishing up her third and final season living in the forest outside of Big Bear, California, at an outdoor science school.

Aimee and Mai-Yan's bike trip lasted four months and was completely self-sustained. Their plan to spend at least one night per week in a hotel ended up being only two hotel stays the whole summer. This made for a lot of camp meals and experimentation with food in the outdoors. When they returned to Los Angeles, all three women were "funemployed," with an arsenal of camp food knowledge to share. They started getting together regularly and built Dirty Gourmet as an outdoor cooking blog.

Dirty Gourmet grew organically from the start, allowing the trio to connect with people in the outdoors in many different ways: they volunteered at trail cleanups, gave lectures at wilderness organizations and retail shops, contributed articles to outdoor and lifestyle magazines, and even dabbled in food production. Today, they focus on catering camping trips and teaching outdoor cooking workshops.

With so much varied outdoor experience among them, the women of Dirty Gourmet have a lot of stories to tell. They aren't all success stories, but learning experiences for sure. As is true for any time spent in the outdoors, they believe that even failures can be positive. Learning from them represents accomplishment and encourages more confidence for future adventures.

For more inspiration, visit www.dirtygourmet.com.

ABOUT THE AUTHORS

Ryan Robert Miller

AIMEE TRUDEAU

Virginia Trudeau

Aimee started cooking as a young teenager, reading her mom's *Bon Appetit* magazines after school and then creating elaborate meals while her parents were still at work. Her obsession with food continued into college where she studied food science.

Aimee's earliest memories involve watching coffee percolate on a camp stove. Camping was a regular weekend activity in her family, always eating well, even if the meals were simple and familiar. Once she started camping as an adult, she began to experiment with more interesting food options. Her four-month bike tour with Mai-Yan in the summer of 2009 inspired her camp cooking creativity and opened her eyes to how different her meals were compared to what other campers were eating.

Aimee loves to experiment with various forms of cooking such as dehydrating, Dutch oven baking, and fermenting. She uses these techniques to fuel new recipes that will fit into her plant-based diet, which brings its own challenges, especially when trying to please finicky five-year-old twins, Asha and Ravi.